THE
UNITED
STATES
IN
NORWEGIAN
HISTORY

CONTRIBUTIONS IN
AMERICAN STUDIES
GREENWOOD PRESS

Publications of
THE AMERICAN INSTITUTE
UNIVERSITY OF OSLO

THE
UNITED
STATES
IN
NORWEGIAN
HISTORY

Sigmund Skard

Contributions in American Studies, Number 26

Publications of the American Institute
University of Oslo

GREENWOOD PRESS
Westport, Connecticut • London, England

UNIVERSITETSFORLAGET
Oslo

For Robert E. Spiller

Library of Congress Cataloging in Publication Data

Skard, Sigmund, 1903-
   The United States in Norwegian history.

   (Contributions in American studies ; no. 26)
(Publications of the American Institute)
   Condensed translation of USA i norsk historie.
   Bibliography: p.
   1. United States--Relations (general) with Norway. 2. Norway--Relations
(general) with the United States. I. Title. II. Series: Oslo. Universitet. Ameri-
kansk Institut. Publications.
E183.8.N6S5513   1976   320.9'481'073   76-5263
ISBN 0-8371-8909-8

Published throughout the world, with the exception of the Nordic countries, by Greenwood Press in the series Contributions in American Studies.
Published simultaneously in the Nordic countries by Oslo University Press
in the series Publications of the American Institute, University of Oslo.

Library of Congress Catalog Card Number: 76-5263
ISBN: 82-00-04972-8 (Universitetsforlaget)
ISBN: 0-8371-8909-8 (Greenwood Press)

First published in 1976

Manufactured in the United States of America

Contents

Contents _____vii

Preface

The Norwegians are one of the smallest nations of Europe. They live at the margin of habitable regions and through most of their history have had limited material resources. In spite of such handicaps, they early established contacts with the rest of the world, even across the Atlantic. Since 1776 the United States has influenced Norwegian development in almost all walks of life more deeply than has any other nation outside of Europe. The relationship early showed traits of its own.

If, so far, nobody has tried to follow these contacts through history, it is partly due to the difficulty of the task. The material is extensive, widely scattered, and heterogeneous. It is sometimes difficult to distinguish between the American impact and other influences; even more difficult is distinguishing between such influences and parallel developments. The knowledge, image, and imitation or rejection of America often have a touch of the intangible; opinion research is a slippery field. And, for obvious reasons, Norwegian scholarship long was focused on national subjects. American studies were a late development.

Nevertheless, European investigation of the American impact on Europe early threw light upon the influence on Norway. The first attempt at a general survey was made by a Norwegian scholar, Halvdan Koht, in *The American Spirit in Europe* (1949). One important feature of this history was thoroughly analyzed from the American point of view in Theodore C. Blegen's *Norwegian Migration to America* (1931-1940) and from the Norwegian in Ingrid Semmingsen's *Veien mot vest* (Westward Course) (1942-1950). At the same time, Reidar Öksnevad published his bibliography, *U.S.A. in Norwegian Literature* (1950), which covered the years to 1946. Twenty years later, Jörund Mannsaaker surveyed the emigration motif in Norwegian creative writing (1971). In my own book *American Studies in Europe* (1958), there is also much material relevant to Norway. Among the publications from the American Institute in Oslo were Halvdan Koht's book, already mentioned, and Einar Haugen's *The Norwegian Language in America* (1953). In the series *Americana Norvegica,* published since 1966, a number of specialized studies were devoted to the subject. The present book is an attempt at a summary.

The theme is limited. Norwegian contacts with America before 1776 are of historical importance and are treated briefly, but the real impact began with the foundation of the United States—in this book often called "America" in accordance with common usage. In modern times the traffic has been two-way. Norway has given America more than physical manpower; it may suffice to mention the names of Thorstein Veblen and Henrik Ibsen. But that's a different story.

The book originally was planned as a recapitulation of previous research. But, outside the fields of emigration and belles lettres, it soon proved necessary to base the account to a considerable extent on original investigation. This work was bound to be uneven and, at times, superficial, offering spot checks more often than documentation—increasingly so after 1914, when the material becomes both colossal and unwieldy. Repeatedly, I was also forced into fields where my lack of competence could not be camouflaged. The compensatory emphasis on the history of ideas and literature is, however, partly justified by the historical facts. Much of the contact between the two nations has been other than material.

The book could not have been written without the brilliant spade work of the pioneer scholars mentioned above. Also, with the support of the Norwegian Research Council, much material has been collected in recent years, successively by Ingrid Semmingsen, Egil Tveteraas, and Öyvind Gulliksen, who all have done a first-rate job. A special debt of gratitude is owed to Professor Arlow W. Andersen of Wisconsin State University, who placed at my disposal a detailed survey, printed only in part, of American political news in the Norwegian press from 1875 to 1905.

In addition, I was able to discuss the work in progress with friends, who gave me the benefit of their criticism. In particular should be mentioned my Norwegian colleagues Ingrid Semmingsen, Torbjörn Sirevaag, my wife Aase Gruda Skard, Sverre Steen, and Stein Tveite. The University Library in Oslo assisted the research indefatigably.

The bulk of the original material, with extensive documentation and bibliography, is being presented simultaneously in a more comprehensive work in Norwegian, under the title *USA i norsk historie* (Oslo, Det Norske Samlaget, 1976), of which the present book is a condensed translation. Most of the sources are written in Norwegian, and many of them are available only in the Oslo University Library. A system of references in footnotes would be extremely bulky and actually of little help. This English version therefore contains only a bibliography of the most essential sources, with emphasis on those written in English. Scholars who would like to go more deeply into the subject are referred to the Norwegian edition. The chapters on Björnstjerne Björnson and Halvdan Koht have appeared in print in slightly different versions in the collection *Abroad in America: Visitors to the New Nation, 1776-1914* (National Portrait Gallery, Washington, D.C., 1976), and the chapter on H. Tambs Lyche in abbreviated form in *The Norway-America Association Year Book 1975* (Oslo, 1975).

The publication of the English version was subsidized by the Norwegian Ministry of Foreign Affairs and by the United States Information Agency, Oslo. The manuscript was typed by my longtime secretary, Else Bjerke Westre, was read for content by Professor Robert H. Walker, and finally copy edited by Ann Santoro. I am deeply grateful for their assistance.

The book is focused on facts and trends that presumably are of more general interest. For that and for other reasons, the account is sketchy and fragmentary. But it is hoped that, in spite of its short-comings, the survey may give the foreign reader an impression of the importance of the United States in the growth of the Norwegian nation and of the strong emotions and varied ideas which it has provoked during the many centuries when Norwegians have crossed the Atlantic in ships and airplanes, thoughts and dreams.

This volume is respectfully and affectionately dedicated to Robert E. Spiller, Professor Emeritus at Swarthmore and the University of Pennsylvania, and former Visiting Professor at Oslo. Thirty years ago, he encouraged me to enter the field of American Studies. He became my first teacher, has ever since remained my powerful and faithful adviser, collaborator, helper, and friend, and has been the same to countless scholars all around the world.

§

THE
UNITED
STATES
IN
NORWEGIAN
HISTORY

CHAPTER 1

The Shores of Vinland 1000-1500

During the Middle Ages, Norsemen not only built a realm of considerable stability and cultural standards at home but also displayed a surprising expansiveness abroad. They plundered widely in Western Europe. They founded a kingdom in Ireland and established long-lasting settlements in Scotland, the Scottish and Faroe isles, Iceland, and Greenland. As the farthest ramification of this movement, they were also the first Europeans in historic times to set foot on the American continent, around A.D. 1000.

The Norse expedition to America was mentioned for the first time more than two generations later by a German historian, Adam from Bremen in what is the oldest appearance of America in literature. During the following two centuries, there are only scattered references in Icelandic sources; the manuscripts of the most important reports are of considerably later date. Thus, they contain a good deal of legendary material, but the story itself has a strong internal truth. Chronology is consistent, with five expeditions between the years 1000 and 1015. Astronomical, geographical, botanical, and ethnographical details make it probable that what the Norsemen called Helleland, Markland, and Vinland must have been located somewhere near St. Lawrence Bay or on Labrador. Later, the explorers may also have reached New England. Confirmation came in 1960 when Norwegian excavations on Newfoundland brought to light the sites of houses that date from the period and, beyond any doubt, are of Norse origin.

In the present context, however, the details of the Vinland voyages have less interest than the impression which they made. Modern writing and art have lent to these expeditions a romantic grandeur which Leiv Eiriksson and his men would not have felt. Norsemen were accustomed to landings on strange shores around the grim northern oceans. They could have had no real idea of the continent that they had come upon.

Nevertheless, the discovery doubtless had a touch of the extraordinary. The narrative, as pieced together from the sagas, is captivating and filled with emotion. To us, it also carries some far-reaching omens of the future. The Vinland of the storytellers is sensational, at the same time distant and alluring. Even at this early date, the natives are described as living lives of both primitive simplicity and savagery. Above all, there is the richness of the new land: a milder climate, self-sown cereals, unknown fruits, and an opulence of venison, fowl, and fish (precious metals are not yet noted). "People talked of the voyage to Vinland," says the narrator, "because this seemed to be an open road to wealth and honor." There was going to be much traffic along that road in centuries to come, and for the same purpose.

The all-important fact about Vinland is, however, that it remained a fleeting glimpse, an episode. When the Indians resisted attempts at colonization, the Norsemen lacked the necessary military strength and technique to prevail. There is no sign that they penetrated from the coastal rim; the famous "runic stone" from Kensington, Minn., is a modern hoax. The Norsemen came from Greenland, where living conditions were tough, indeed, and left little surplus for a continued effort. There were scattered later sailings to Labrador, largely for driftwood, but apparently no further attempts at colonization. The advanced base in Greenland also proved to be untenable. As the climate deteriorated, survival became increasingly difficult for the Norsemen there. Their only salvation would have been closer contact with their homeland, but, toward the end of the Middle Ages, the Norwegian realm itself came into a period of political and economic decay. Communications with Greenland broke down. Left alone, the Norse population in the colony deteriorated physically until the Eskimos penetrated from the north and replaced them.

Possibly, the memory of Vinland survived among Norsemen during the following centuries, but we have no reports to that effect. The same oblivion prevails outside of the Nordic countries. It is uncertain whether the Vinland voyages were known to the great sailors who steered westward from Spain toward the end of the fifteenth century. America had to be rediscovered, even by Norsemen.

§

CHAPTER 2

The Second Discovery 1500- 1750

"The Fourth Part of the World"

When in 1492 the boats of Christopher Columbus grated against the beach sand of the Bahamas, he had not found old India but the New World, which soon was to cause great changes in the Old.

The discovery resulted in an immense movement of colonization among powers large and small. The expansion stimulated social upheaval. The riches of the New World made themselves felt in economic life. New cultural products began to penetrate Europe.

The intellectual impact worked even more deeply. The Americas fostered in the mind of the Old World the long-lasting dream of El Dorado, the transatlantic never-never land of swift and uncontrolled material gain. The natives, their Arcadian innocence faced with the destructiveness of Christian barbarism, raised somber philosophical questions of human nature and behavior. The British colonies on the East Coast still had little part in these momentous happenings, but the problems were general and were discussed everywhere.

For two centuries, Norway was almost completely bypassed by these developments. In its weakness, it had drifted into unions with the other Nordic countries and by 1500 had become a part of the Danish realm, a situation that was to last until 1814. For all practical purposes, the Norwegian state was obliterated. Both Danes and Swedes participated in the colonization of America; Norway had neither the political nor economic power necessary. As yet, Norwegian shipping hardly ever reached across the Atlantic. Culturally, the nation was almost totally dependent on Denmark, and its foreign contacts were largely second-hand.

Some intellectual curiosity existed, however, and after 1500 was encouraged by the spirit of humanism with its interest in the national past. The scholars in Oslo had studied in Copenhagen and at the universities of Northern Germany, where the New World was still far off; indeed, its discovery is never mentioned in their writings. But in the western shipping town of Bergen, memories remained of the proud past when Norse settlers occupied Greenland, which reportedly was connected with the new-found "fourth part of the world." Around 1600, Icelanders, Norwegians, and Danes wrote about old Vinland, which "reaches all the way to the Straits of Magellan and must be inhabited by sundry kinds of people." Norwegian scholars reminded the Danish king of the riches which the Spaniards had gained across the ocean and encouraged him to search for the same regions by way of Greenland, and several attempts to do so were made.

Real knowledge of America was to remain extremely meager for a long time, however. Norwegian scholarship of the seventeenth century, dominated by theology and abstruse learning, was largely preoccupied with the native religions of the new continent. A doctoral dissertation even tried to prove that Christianity had been preached in America long before Columbus. In 1686 a patriotic poet maintained that the marvelous Norsemen had "sown their noble seed" all over the New World and had been expelled only by the Spaniards.

But gradually there was a change of atmosphere in Norway. The nation slowly regained its strength. A ruling class of officials became the vanguard of new intellectual life. Isolation began breaking down. Norwegians participated in the great European wars of the period and traveled around the world. German dominance in cultural life was weakened. The first handbooks of the English language in the Dano-Norwegian realm were produced by Norwegians. There were also the beginnings of direct contact across the ocean. The Danish crown acquired the Virgin Islands as a colony. The West Indies soon became a commercial point of contact with the entire New World; even Norwegian shipping tried to gain a foothold there. The results still were modest. Very few ships made the journey, and few American products reached Norway except for tobacco, syphilis, and "the New England method of preserving dried codfish." But some personal contacts were established. Between the years 1630 and 1674, about sixty Norwegians settled in the state of New York, mostly after service in the British or Dutch navy—portents of more to come.

The New Century

It was the eighteenth century which opened Norway to the world, and the motive power was intellectual. The new ideas of the Enlightenment made their entrance with their skeptical rationalism and realism. Even in Norway there was now a larger reading public, open to fresh impulses. Their inquisitiveness was to extend to the New World as well.

In scholarship, new winds were blowing westward. The Icelander Thormod Torfason lived in Norway from the 1670s as royal historiographer. He not only encouraged national pride by his huge *History of the Norwegian Kings* but also competently discussed the old Norse discovery in his *History of Old Vinland* (1705). The book was written in Latin, reached the entire learned world, and appeared in American translation as late as 1891.

There were other stimuli. From the year 1721 onward, the Norwegian clergyman Hans Egede undertook his heroic new colonization of Greenland. Interest extended to the past of the entire new continent. A Norwegian woman in 1747 found many readers for her translation of a Spanish book on the conquest of Mexico.

The British settlements in North America also gradually piqued curiosity. These settlements were still in their pioneering period. They offered few sensations and as yet had no political or intellectual importance. They were still undiscovered by the enlightened "philosophers" of Europe. But the Norwegians had material reasons for their interest: for instance, Americans were active in the main fields of Norwegian export, lumber and fish. In Norwegian handbooks of geography from the first decades after 1700, surely five times as many pages are devoted to the regions of America south of the Rio Grande than to the rest of the continent. But there is decent information about landscape, climate, and resources in the British colonies as well, including tobacco (the "Virginian incense"), and a particular preoccupation with the religious "independents," the Quakers and William Penn.

The intellectual pioneer in the field was the historian and playwright Ludvig Holberg (1684-1754), the first Norwegian to take a decisive part in the cultural life of the Danish and Norwegian nations. In his own intellectual development, Holberg turned away from the learned obsession with the past to the life of his own age, particularly in England and France. He absorbed the new ideas less as a system than as an attitude, secular and critical, seeking the real values of civilization. In the immense bulk of his writing, America itself still played a minor part. But his approach is significant.

Holberg cared nothing for the Old Norse "buccaneers" and the writers who found "Norse colonies in all parts of the world." In his comedies, he demonstrated with a smile how strange and distant the New World still was to his simple fellow-countrymen in contemporary Copenhagen. In his numerous historical works, he was particularly interested in Latin America. But the details are telling. He did not believe in a primitive paradise. To him, the natives were distinguished by "immorality and ignorance." He was equally unimpressed by the Christian "conversions."

In this context, Holberg also mentioned New England once in a while—the foundation of the colonies, and their important commerce. As yet, he saw nothing in these parts that called for special admiration. That the British in America represented any form of popular government did not occur to him, nor would he have liked such a thing. He saw nothing in America to support Montesquieu's theory that a temperate climate is favorable to liberty. He explicitly disapproved of some aspects of New England civilization. The Quakers to him were "ridiculous fanatics."

Thus, it was not Holberg's knowledge of America that was trail-breaking, but his general attitude. Undauntedly, he measured the New World with his own yardstick and saw it in the context of his own ideas. Others were going to follow him along the same road.

§

CHAPTER 3

The Enlightened Atlantis 1750- 1807

Diminishing Distance

Until the middle of the eighteenth century, the American impact on Norway remained superficial. But from that time onward, America gradually took on a new role in history, with effects noticeable everywhere.

Increasingly through the century, the ideas of the Enlightenment had come to dominate intellectual life in Europe; on them were based the demands of the bourgeois class for the "natural" rights of liberty. But these ideals had not yet found a striking national symbol. The "philosophers" toyed with a number of peoples about whom they knew pleasantly little, from the Chinese, the Incas, and the Swiss to Jesuit Paraguay and the Corsica of Pascal Paoli. They even wrote of the classical simplicity of the American Indians. But the idea did not work. The "philosophers" were not really primitivists.

At the middle of the century, however, the problem was solved by a feat of intellectual acrobatics whereby the dream of the "noble

Indian" was transferred to the cultivated British settlers in America, heirs to the traditions of old, free England. From 1730 onward, Voltaire began to make the "good American Quaker" the carrier of all his ideals. From about 1770, this image was quietly enlarged to comprise all of the British colonists, creating a kind of "many-sided Indian-Greek-Roman-American idol." The American Revolution and the Declaration of Independence proved the dream to be true beyond any expectations. The ensuing war soon became international. After little more than a decade, the American Revolution was directly succeeded by the even more momentous upheaval in France.

Instrumental in the process of identification was that matchless practical psychologist Benjamin Franklin. In his homely fur cap, he exemplified in the salons of Paris the new democratic man incarnate, messenger from a society where nature and culture were happily married. In European minds, he was soon to be joined by the noble George Washington, the ideal combination of citizen, warrior, and statesman. The two, and their nation, became the subject of a "secular mysticism," which spread all over Europe with lightning speed. In the words of Mme. de Staël, America represented "the vanguard of mankind."

With the swift development of the French Revolution into a reign of terror, these sentiments were bound to change. As European reaction organized its resistance, events themselves created a negative counter-image of America as the homeland of a radical poison. At another extreme, the idol lost its power for an opposite reason: Franklin was no real revolutionist! But to moderates of all descriptions, the American "revolution without guillotines" now came to appear as quite acceptable. Napoleon confirmed the image, a "son of the Revolution" and at the same time a spokesman of law and order, wrapped in George Washington's Roman toga.

For special reasons, these ideas found a particularly fertile soil in Norway. Its swiftly growing bourgeois class eagerly absorbed "enlightened" ideas. Even before the American Revolution, there was an increasing number of indications that Norwegian readers closely followed international debate even with regard to America. But these reports from far away were to acquire a special relevance in Norway because of growing discontent there.

By 1770 the Norwegians were generally complaining about the

expensive and burdensome Danish administration. They demanded a higher degree of independence and some national institutions of their own. Such tendencies were particularly evident among the Norwegian students in Copenhagen. They were egged on by the national historian Gerhard Schöning, who proudly described how his Viking forefathers had "liberated the subjugated nations of Europe from the Roman slavery" and "undisputedly" had extended their activity even to North America. This new assurance was behind the first Norwegian national anthem, written in 1772 and forbidden by the Danish police, with its rebellious appeal "to break the chains of oppression." Norwegians were well prepared when, four years later, Americans broke *their* chains.

In the first instance, however, the effect in Norway of the American Revolution was practical. For the first time, that distant country became something to be reckoned with by the average Norwegian in his daily life. Denmark-Norway was neutral in the war, but quite a few Norwegians participated on both sides. A leading Dano-Norwegian naval officer fought with distinction under the French flag and was present when Cornwallis surrendered at Yorktown. Such contacts hardly remained unknown. More important, neutrality proved to create a golden age for Norwegian transatlantic shipping and export, which served both sides in the struggle. During the war the Norwegian merchant marine was almost doubled in size. Some Norwegian ships even "carried Hessian mercenaries to the bloody fields of George Washington."

Norwegian sympathy was, however, strongly on the side of the Americans because they maintained the principle of free shipping against the British. In 1779 an American frigate took three English prize ships into the Norwegian port of Bergen. At that time the Danish government had not yet recognized the United States and "with great pain" felt obliged to give the vessels up to the British. But the citizens of Bergen protested against this decision.

There were also more peaceful connections. Quite a number of Norwegians now served in the Danish administration in Westindia, and some achieved renown. One of them even became governor general and married the daughter of John Jacob Astor. Some emigration continued to the British colonies; around 1750 a small group of Norwegian Herrnhutians settled at Bethlehem, Pa.

But under normal conditions, direct business between Norway

and the United States still remained insignificant. The only article to speak of was the fish which went to the West Indies. Norwegian shipping to those parts increased slightly after 1800. In 1806, fifteen ships sailed from Bergen to the Danish colonies, but since Norway then had about 1,100 seagoing vessels and Bergen alone 228, the figure is not impressive.

More important was the appearance of new American cultural products. Norwegian papers published the first notices about American technical inventions. But the real impact was in agriculture. The American potato soon became a staple commodity in Norway. Although the use of corn never got beyond the stage of discussion, American trees were highly recommended, and timothy grass soon became common in Norwegian meadows. The first Norwegian book on American natural history was a learned work (1797) on the botany of the West Indies.

"The Sons of Liberty"

Beginning with the Revolution, however, a major American influence became one of ideas. The French immigrant Hector de Crèvecoeur, who was also known in Norway, wrote around 1780 that a distinguishing feature of America was its "close affinity with our present time." That characteristic was going to persist.

The American Revolution marks the beginning of a general radicalization of Europe. The Norwegians well knew that the French had followed an American example. But within the Dano-Norwegian monarchy, reaction to these developments showed significant differences. In Denmark, the effect was blunted by important reforms which the government carried through at the time. Norwegians did not feel quite the same way. They still asked in vain for a university and a national bank. Their economic life worked at a considerable disadvantage; there were even some serious riots. There was a growing sense of national identity. The idea of the sovereignty of the people was bound to find more open minds in Norway than across the Skagerrak.

Such sentiments now were nourished by more abundant information from abroad. Norwegian papers still were poor, but most members of the educated classes read the brilliant Danish journal *Minerva*. Two of its leading editors were Norwegians, and they were radicals. From the very beginning, they greeted the French Revolution as a natural reaction to "the most intolerable oppression." (They both eventually had to leave their positions and died in the West Indies.) In another Danish journal in the 1790s, the Norwegians could read, through ten volumes, translations of the most important writings of Thomas Paine.

As a result, there was much rebellious discussion among Norwegians both in Copenhagen and at home. In many places people got together, "talked revolution," and worshipped France, "Liberty and Republicanism." The most audacious even maintained the legality of "an insurrection undertaken by an entire nation" against "royalists, aristocrats and similar rascals." Such outbursts often were accompanied by obsequious expressions of loyalty to the fatherly Dano-Norwegian monarch. But doubtless they bear witness to a slightly different attitude toward America as compared to that of the Danes. Significant also is Norwegian interest in other nations idolized by "enlightened" writers: the Swiss, the Latin American Jesuits, and the Corsicans. A Norwegian clergyman in 1770 even had the idea of baptizing his son "Pascal Paoli."

But if America proved much more attractive to Norwegians than other nations, it was because of their own special situation, which gave to that country an emotional note of its own. Many Norwegians at the time hated England, the "new Carthage." But others, particularly of the merchant class, had served their apprenticeship in England, loved British traditions, and recognized them in the new America. There was also a geographical parallel between the American rebels and the Norwegians. Finnish libertarians, rising in the 1780s against mighty Sweden across the ocean, saw the Americans as their own counterparts. Some Norwegians may have harbored similar feelings in relation to the Danes.

This new interest did not yet in Norway give birth to scholarly works about America, as was the case, for instance, in contemporary Sweden. As yet, no Norwegian author had visited the United States. We know the contents of more than one hundred private Norwegian libraries between the years 1750 and 1800; there is hardly one single American book. Even the discussions in Norwegian newspapers and journals are often relatively poor, but these day-to-day judgments are highly instructive when it comes to public opinion, and sometimes they show a good deal of acumen.

In the beginning, there was no blind worship of America, as is evidenced by the writings of the leading Norwegian journalist of the period, Claus Fasting. His journal, *Provinzial-Blade* (1778-1781), touched upon many of the main ideas of future discussion. Fasting was well aware of the absorbing interest his readers had in anything American and devoted a good deal of space to such news. In particular, he printed an extensive eulogy of the Quaker state of Pennsylvania. But he judged with a critical eye the real aims of the insurgents in the War of Independence. He was somewhat disturbed by the prospect of their economic and military might in the future. He even openly warned against some aspects of American democracy: "too much liberty is no liberty."

The Danish *Minerva,* a decade later, also spoke frankly about American shortcomings. But as a whole the songs of praise became ever more frequent; negative reports about America largely were described as the fruits of envy. This increase of sympathy appears to have been general. "God help the American *sons of liberty*," wrote a Norwegian clergyman in 1782, "lest all mankind perish in serfdom. My delight by the news of Cornwallis' captivity is unbelievable."

"The Ideal of Human Perfection"

As the eighteenth century moved toward its close and the Old World increasingly was swept by turmoil, the positive image of the United States became more elaborate. It was expressed strikingly by poets and writers. An example is Professor Niels Treschow (1751-1833), Norway's foremost philosopher and, after independence, one of its first ministers of education. In a poem written at the threshold of the new century, he saw a Europe given over to blood and darkness, with many reasons for misgivings. But there is one glimmer of hope: America exists, "high by its past deeds, even higher by its expectations," lest we should altogether despair about the future of humanity. "What liberty, industry and enlightenment can accomplish has been proved by the USA."

In Norway, as all over Europe, the personal symbols of this vision were the twin idols, Washington and Franklin. In classical simplification they expressed the aspirations of the time. They were repeatedly compared to Greek and Roman heroes and were surrounded by the same veneration: nobody "has come closer to the ideal of human perfection." Franklin, above all, appealed to Norwegian imagination with his unbelievable versatility and his soberminded idealism. Youngsters expressed in moving words how the Philadelphian had become an ethical power in their lives.

The great examples were put to use in education for citizenship. Textbooks for Norwegian schools expressed a feeling of sympathy and fellowship toward Americans, and the message went out even to less sophisticated classes. A book from the year 1800, published "as an encouraging example to honest peasants and craftsmen," contains four biographies: those of Franklin, the Norwegian "apostle of Greenland" Hans Egede, Columbus, and William Penn.

As time moved on, more negative traits crept into the picture. American mistreatment of Negroes and Indians was noted. There were reports about a moneyed aristocracy, land speculation, imperfect administration of justice, dissension, licentiousness, and even anarchy in America before the adoption of the federal Constitution. But there was a willingness to see things from the best side. Norwegians, too, were acquainted with the widespread notion of the time that climate in America was bound to lead to a physical deterioration. But it was maintained that such conditions might largely have reference to the tropical regions, not to North America, which was "in the rise of its grandeur." There was little in Norway of the conservative tendency, widespread, for example, in contemporary Sweden, to turn America into a somber image of warning.

This attitude was increasingly strengthened through the 1790s by the sanguinary developments in France: the American Revolution was different. George Washington remained an ideal even in that regard: he "never used wanton words to the princes of Europe and never saw himself as an apostle of liberty, proselyting all over the world." The republican Franklin "does not think at all about the subversion in France as do many subjects of monarchs."

The conflicting tendencies are brought out clearly in the many references to Thomas Paine. To some writers, he was the despicable spokesman of "the fanaticism of liberty," to others, the "noble friend of man." *Minerva* in 1793 put him nicely in his place: his work was "beneficient in North America at his time, disastrous in the France of our day."

Behind this caution on the part of Norwegians there was also a realistic sense of moderation and the middle road, which had been strong in Ludvig Holberg and was also dominant in the leading Norwegian writers of the time. Such tempered enthusiasm for America, with its typical qualifications, was clearly expressed by the statesman and jurist Envold Falsen (1755-1808). In his youth he praised the urge for "liberty on the entire earth," but in the 1790s he made it clear that freedom could be built only on moral qualities, which were summed up in the word "civism" (the virtue of the citizen) and might well be found in monarchies, just as it had sometimes been lacking in parliamentary England. Americans had solved the problem on their virgin soil, not because of their republican institutions, not even because of their leadership, but because of that "deliberate courage" and "philosophical calm" which was immortalized in George Washington and made his America the positive counterpart to the French revolution.

A fitting vignette to end this chapter is provided by the figure of Bernt Anker (1746-1805). At the turn of the century, he was Norway's leading businessman, Maecenas, bel esprit, and social lion. Of all the works of music, art, and literature that adorned the parties at his mansion in Christiania, the climax was always the performance of his own plays in the grand style. He himself regarded as his masterpiece the drama *Major André*, based on a real person in the American War of Independence, a collaborator of Benedict Arnold who was eventually hanged as a British spy.

The play was never printed, and not much is lost thereby. But André's part was played by Bernt Anker himself "with truth and nature," and the other parts by a group of his guests. Through the mouths of George Washington and his fellow insurgents, these ladies and gentlemen from the highest society in Christiania proclaimed that they worked for "the liberty of the millions" against "the horrid yoke of tyrants" and in defense of the "sacred treasures granted us by Nature."

The play was performed several times, but most memorably in 1788, in the presence of the Dano-Norwegian crown prince himself, the later King Frederik VI. Neither the author, the actors, the aristo-cratic audience, nor the heir to the Dano-Norwegian absolute mon-archy apparently found anything strange in the program of this gala performance.

§

CHAPTER 4

Ally Behind the Ocean 1807-1814

War and Reconsideration

Until the year 1807, the game of the great powers had made it possible for the Norwegians to cultivate their economic interests and their theoretical sympathy for the United States peacefully within the walls of Dano-Norwegian neutrality. During the seven years that followed, this framework was broken by the same powers.

It was Napoleon who knocked the chessmen down. In order to break his main adversary, Great Britain, he demanded of all the continental governments that they join him in a total blockade of the British isles. The Danish regent, Frederik VI (king from 1808), much preferred to follow the French emperor. But war with England would have meant catastrophe to the Norwegian part of his realm. When he hesitated too long, the British did not dare to wait. In 1807 they attacked Copenhagen and captured the large Dano-Norwegian fleet.

The ensuing war with Great Britain placed the Norwegians in a completely new position. Norway got most of its grain across the ocean from Denmark and paid for it by its shipping on the seven seas. The war and the blockade meant economic ruin, starvation, disease, and death. To most Norwegians, the war must have appeared senseless, and even more so the following war with Sweden, England's ally.

For all practical purposes, Norway was now cut off from Denmark. Reluctantly, the king had to recognize a local government and, finally, allow the establishment of a Norwegian university. But it was too late. The idea of independence grew in strength. Norwegians felt that their interests were being sacrificed. They defended themselves well both against the British and the Swedes, and their success created a new self-confidence. Still, few Norwegians envisaged a total breach with Denmark. But they planned for an extensive self-government which would incorporate new forms. Even Norwegian officials of the autocratic state now began wondering whether the people shouldn't be granted more political power.

America already had its place in this world of ideas, and the war with England brought it even more into the field of vision. But, as before, immediate practical consequences were predominant in the beginning.

The war was, in the first place, a merciless war against commerce. None of the neutrals had resisted the British rule of the waves more strongly than the Americans. The Norwegians were bound to follow them even more sympathetically now, since they themselves were openly fighting Albion. Even before the United States officially entered the war, it must have appeared to Norwegians as a kind of unofficial ally. Norwegian papers of the time gave enthusiastic reports about the Americans, who, in William Pitt's words, "preferred poverty in freedom to golden chains." The captains of American prize-ships told how well they were received in Norwegian ports. The admiral of the Norwegian navy, who managed to keep the British out of Norwegian waters, was the same man who, some decades before, had fought them at Yorktown.

As the war progressed, even more unusual connections developed. In all countries, privateering became an essential part of warfare, a legalized piracy, based on an unbelievable tangle of sophistic rules.

After the loss of its navy, Norway equipped hundreds of such privateers. The neutral United States now had merchant ships on all of
the oceans, and the rules offered them scant protection. Soon, the
majority of prize-ships taken into Norwegian ports were American.

In 1809 John Quincy Adams happened to visit the center of Norwegian privateering, the harbor of Christianssand, on the way to
his post as American ambassador in St. Petersburg. There he found
almost thirty American prize-ships with their crews. Through Adams's
influence, a citizen of the town was appointed the first American
consul to Norway in order to assist them. In fact, Americans for
various reasons were treated more than leniently by the Norwegian
prize courts. On the average, only every fifth ship was confiscated.
Nevertheless, even America unwillingly contributed to the brief
prosperity of the Norwegian coastal cities during the legendary
"prize years."

Onward to Independence

This fleeting interlude might have lasted long if, in the summer of
1812, Napoleon hadn't launched his attack on Russia. Two years
before, the Swedes had elected the French marshal Jean Bernadotte their crown prince under the name Charles John. He made an
agreement with the Russians to join them and the other member
states in the great coalition against Napoleon if, in compensation,
they guaranteed him the conquest of Norway. Napoleon lost his
war against the Russian winter. When his defeat was certain, Charles
John marched northward. By a treaty signed at Kiel in January
1814, King Frederik was forced to cede Norway to Sweden.

In the meantime, the Danish king had sent to Norway as governor
his cousin and successor to the throne, the young Prince Christian
Frederik, hoping that he might save the country for the dynasty.
But the prince found a different Norway. Antipathy toward Denmark was on the increase among the population. Finances were in a
miserable state, and the food situation desperate. Abroad, there
was a general popular rising against Napoleon, the comrade-in-
arms of the Danish king. More and more Norwegians wrote off the
union with Denmark. Some were willing to accept a union with

Sweden; others dreamed of complete independence. In this situation, Norwegian sympathies toward the United States suddenly proved to be a strong political influence.

In a way, the two countries now had reason to feel even closer than before. Since 1812 the United States had been at war with Great Britain, as was Norway itself. Even the Americans now warred mainly by privateering. Their warships visited Norwegian waters, ran into Norwegian harbors, often with British prizes, and were received with the friendliness of "joint cause against joint enemy." But this situation was changed completely by the cession of Norway to Sweden, and so the Norwegians concentrated their powers on reorganizing their own state. American ideas proved to fit in marvelously.

On New Year's day of 1814 a newspaper in Christiania expressed the hope that a powerful leader might now arise in Norway "like Luther or Franklin." But the demands of the situation were soon expressed more specifically. The Danish prince had planned to take over the government of Norway in accordance with his right of succession. He was soon given to understand that the people now demanded a good deal more. Forced by circumstances, the prince called a Constitutional Assembly, to meet in April.

The intervening months saw endless political speculation in all classes of society. Constitutions were drafted everywhere, and existing ones were made available in translation, including those of several American states. Among the more competent planners was a group of citizens in Bergen. They knew most of the modern constitutions, "particularly that of the North American republic," and harbored democratic ideas. One of its members donated to the forthcoming Assembly a comprehensive edition of the American texts.

The individual who had the most profound knowledge in this respect was, however, the young Judge Christian Magnus Falsen (1782-1830), later to become the leading figure of the Assembly. From his father, Envold Falsen, he had absorbed American ideas. All through his life, he studied American history together with the Norwegian history of Gerhard Schöning. The two worlds mingled in his mind: the American form of self-government seemed to have the same sound balance which he believed to have been typical of Old Norse rural society, based on "liberty, equality, and property."

In a biography of George Washington, Falsen described him as the epitome of moral strength, marked by a "serious thoughtfulness" and an "extraordinary self-mastery" and unselfishness based on "the laws of honor and common sense."

The Assembly which convened in April thus had at its disposal considerable knowledge of the work of its American counterpart in 1787. In fact, the two gatherings themselves also had a good deal in common.

Both nations already had tasted some self-government, and their faraway monarchs had removed themselves from office. In neither nation was the reform called forth by internal oppression or old hatred, but rather was the fruit of quiet growth; on both sides of the ocean "the people" was a positive phrase. At the same time, the assemblies representing the people were the expression of the classes of property, the "third estate"; the lower class was left out as a matter of course. They were the spokesmen of balance and moderation. They would now have their share in the political power, but they were not intent on any kind of social revolution. In both places, there was the feeling of a fresh start, based on principles of justice that were felt as a national heritage.

In the Norway of 1814, America could be only one model among many. Much had happened since 1776, events closer and more sensational. Taking such facts into consideration, it is surprising to see how strongly America was present in the minds of Norwegians. The historical situations were felt to be parallel: two small nations were rising heroically against superior forces. There was a similarity of intellectual atmosphere, that spiritual tradition which made Benjamin Franklin and Ludvig Holberg dear to their nations. There was also in the social structure a comparable democratic trend which would appear more clearly in the future.

"The Best Constitutions"

The Constitutional Assembly convened at Eidsvoll, a rural manor in the Norwegian "colonial style," residence of Christian Frederik's closest friend, Carsten Anker (1747-1824).

America was mentioned as a model on the very first day. When, upon arrival, the delegates presented their credentials to the prince, the representative of a small western Norwegian town expressed the hope that the Assembly might succeed in finding "a wise distribution of power between people and regent," such as was known "in England and America." When deliberations began, however, it soon became clear that there was practical unanimity with regard to the principles of the forthcoming constitution, so deeply had the new ideas penetrated. Some kind of democracy was a foregone conclusion, both among the spokesmen for complete independence and among those who might accept a union with Sweden.

The details were left to the Constitutional Committee, which was chaired by Christian Magnus Falsen; also members were two of his friends from Bergen. But probably most of the members were more or less acquainted with the American material, in both its original form and the numerous adaptations in other countries. Among the many private drafts submitted to the committee, several refer to such sources.

Most striking in this regard is the elaborate draft constitution presented by Falsen himself in collaboration with a Danish jurist, J. G. Adler. The general bill of rights in the draft largely combined the French bill of rights of 1793 and corresponding parts of the Massachusetts and New Hampshire constitutions of 1780. The essential sentence, "Laws, not men should govern," was translated from the Massachusetts document.

The draft of the law itself utilized details from a number of European constitutions, adapted to Norwegian demands. But the organization of the legislative power and a number of individual features were borrowed from American models. The draft adopted the British-American jury system, the suspensive veto, and the strong emphasis on the personal immunity of the members of Parliament. Other features were more conservative, expressing Falsen's sense of moderation. Thus, he imitated the American Senate, but turned it into a highly effective braking mechanism, aristocratic and selective, with even the right of veto.

The Constitutional Committee largely followed the Adler-Falsen draft but sometimes added more from American sources, for example, elements regarding the procedure of impeachment and the general accounting office. The jury system was not adopted. Instead, the Senate was made more democratic, closer to its American counterpart. The General Assembly was pleased with the proposal and passed it in the course of seven days. The most important new addition from American sources was a proportional representation of town and countryside, which was not very democratic in regard to Norwegian society of 1814. The Assembly also dropped the general proclamation of religious tolerance, probably out of respect for the Lutheran state church of Norway. A number of controversial details were left for decision in the future.

In these discussions, America was not often mentioned, but in the debate concerning the Senate, there were references to "the best constitutions, the English and American." On the greatest day of the Assembly, when the members heroically accepted the dire financial consequences of the establishment of the new state, two of the representatives pointed to the brave Americans in the War of Independence and their willingness to sacrifice even more heavily.

On the 17th of May the members signed the constitution and elected Prince Christian Frederik to "the throne of the Old Norse kings." Christian Magnus Falsen had been the moving power in the Assembly and had every reason to be pleased with the result. The constitution in its final form was the most liberal in Europe but showed the internal balance that had been Falsen's main intention. Norway had gone through a revolution but had done so with a controlled calm and an orderliness "unparalleled in the history of Europe." The last words were not chosen at random.

At the royal ceremony concluding the session of the Assembly, republican parallels would not have been in place. But Falsen was not only the father of the constitution. On the same day he also celebrated a more private event: a son was christened. On that occasion he did not choose a Roman, French, or Old Norse name, not even "Christian Frederik," but had the boy baptized "George Benjamin."

Victory in Defeat

Eidsvoll was marked by the high hopes of springtime. The fall mood was more sober.

Two weeks after Eidsvoll, Christian Magnus Falsen published a pamphlet about the prospects of the new state and pointed to the great models abroad, among them the Americans: "For seven years they fought against the terrible odds. Not in vain, brethren, should these gorgeous examples shine before our eyes!" Falsen's hope, and that of the newly elected king, was that the great powers should break their promise to Charles John. But these calculations went wrong, and then the conclusion was foregone. After a brief and hopeless war with the Swedes, Christian Frederik was forced to abdicate and return to Denmark. In November, Parliament elected Charles John king of Norway.

Through the war and the tough negotiations that followed, the Norwegians nevertheless managed to save the most important gain of the year, the free constitution. Historically speaking, that prosaic battle was as decisive as the creative rapture of the spring months. But in our context that chapter is bound to be short. America played a part in the early months of the year, but in the autumn it receded into the background.

Christian Frederik well knew that the fate of free Norway would be decided outside the country itself. From the beginning of the year, he tried to reach the governments of the great powers with friendly proclamations, above all Great Britain: "nobody else can save us from Sweden," Carsten Anker wrote to him. In that light, the United States was now of peripheral interest. The country surely was at war with England all through the year. But it could not be expected to be especially interested in Norway's future position, let alone lend the country any kind of assistance.

Apparently, Christian Frederik did not even intend to notify the Americans of Norway's new position, as he did with the European powers. Instead, he immediately played up to England by closing Norwegian harbors to all privateers. Prizes forthwith would be returned to their homelands. This measure, of course, would hurt mainly the Americans, who were still at war with Great Britain. The American consul pointed this out to Christian Frederik and emphasized the importance of future good relations with the United States. In reply, the king ordered the new rules to be practiced leniently. He also formally notified President Madison of recent happenings in Norway and added an expression of friendly hopes of useful commercial communications. But he would not cancel the ban on privateering; on this point Norway would forthwith adhere to "the strictest principles of neutrality."

Thus, England remained the single hope of Christian Frederik; he sent there the best negotiator available, Carsten Anker, a man of dogged perseverance, which proved to be a necessary asset.

Anker's task appeared hopeless. There was a good deal of sympathy for Norway's cause among the English, particularly in those oppositional circles that, some decades ago, had sided with the American rebels. Leading liberals spoke for Norway in the House of Commons, and so did parts of the press. An English poetess sent Christian Frederik her versified hopes that the waves of the Atlantic might soon "lave the coasts of freedom on either side." But Anker had to operate with utmost caution. The United States, Great Britain's adversary, of course was taboo both to him and to the opposition in Parliament. The British government inflexibly stuck to the promises given Charles John and barely suffered Anker's presence.

At the end of his mission, Anker wrote that nobody would be able to explain what he had "sacrificed and endured" in London. However, his effort was not all in vain. He early discovered that neither Great Britain nor Russia was eager to see Norway and Sweden unified too tightly. Under the circumstances, nobody could have saved the throne of Christian Frederik. But when the war with the Swedes ended up in a tolerable compromise, with the free constitution unscathed, one of the reasons was the British government's insistence on moderation, since Norwegian resistance obviously was more than just a royal machination. This stand was not taken without influence from the opposition in England itself, to which even Anker had contributed. Norway had lost several battles but had actually won the war.

The "marvelous year" was symbolically concluded when, in December, the deputies from the Norwegian Parliament were received at the Swedish royal court. Fascinated contemporary reporters described in detail the glittering company of cavaliers and ladies-in-waiting arrayed for the occasion, all in grand toilettes and full-dress uniforms, and the unembarrassed entrance of the Norwegians with their "extremely modest garments and straightforward manners."

It may be doubted that any of these good Norwegian delegates re-membered, at that moment, Benjamin Franklin's first appearance in 1776 at the court in Versailles, "in his simple outfit among all the powder puffs of Paris." We, at our historic distance, may be allowed to see in the situation a parallel not devoid of meaning.

§

CHAPTER 5

The Opening of a Continent 1815- 1861

In 1814 Norway was carried to its freedom on the waves of the Enlightenment and the general movements of revolution. But when it happened, those waves were already receding. The popular risings against Napoleon were swiftly pacified by the counterrevolution, organized by the "Holy Alliance."

The United States was a symbol of everything the Alliance was fighting. In the period following 1814, the country was not much in the limelight, but from the 1820s onward revolutionary ideas spread anew, climaxed in the upheavals of 1830 and 1848. Once again the United States became an ally of the radicals, its sympathies openly expressed. Free America, in Garibaldi's words, was "a bulwark against European despotism."

The old ideas were given a fresh edge by internal developments which created a totally new America. During the fifty years up to the Civil War, the western portion of the continent opened its immense expanses, and all mankind was invited to share in its riches. The void was filled unbelievably fast by the largest population movement in history. With the same improbable speed, heterogeneous millions were wedded into an orderly mass democracy, with a freedom of movement, a social equality, and a youthful sense of power unparalleled in history. Emigration tied this wonderland to the Old World with a new intimacy. America was no longer an idea of philosophers but a reality to the common man, open particularly to him. Cultural products of many kinds soon proved the fertility of the virgin soil. Here, wrote Goethe, comes something fresh and hopeful, different from the ruined castles of Europe.

But this new America also differed radically from the "classical" rural society of George Washington and gave support to old European misgivings. Frontier America was not only free but crude, wild, and lawless as well; Jacksonian democracy early had a touch of mob rule. The riches of the new continent created a materialism and greed more unrestrained than in the Old World. American popular culture had a touch of the vulgar and life itself a note of the grotesque, soon to be proclaimed to the world as "typically American" by a host of priggish British travelers. Even more ominous was the mushroom growth of American industry. The North went through a development pointing toward "English conditions," with an economic inequality and a brutalized type of existence no more attractive than the planter society of the South, and had within it the seeds of violent internal conflict.

European liberals felt deeply disappointed by this America, doubly because the same tendencies were often manifest in Europe itself. From the 1830s onward, we find in the Old World the first expressions of fear of "Yankeeization" and "Americanization." These hesitations were brought out with classical clarity in Alexis de Tocqueville's great work on American democracy (1835-1840), in which the ambivalence of the author is no less striking than his objectivity.

Norway: The First Decade

During the period immediately following the establishment of its independence, Norway's powers were all-absorbed in the struggle to maintain the gains of 1814. The Swedish king had reluctantly accepted the free constitution but was determined to curtail its democratic liberties; in 1816 he joined the Holy Alliance. Only with difficulty were his attempts repulsed. Distant America was of little relevance in these conflicts. Commercial interrelations with the United States were gradually regulated, but practical consequences were small; shipping had been knocked out by the war. As late as 1838 only one Norwegian ship arrived in New York.

Cultural contacts were no more impressive. Norwegian views of America still have to be gauged largely from the newspapers, which remained extremely poor. But if put together, their meager reports nevertheless add up to a consistent picture: as before, America was a symbol of Eidsvoll and the free constitution, as opposed to reactionary Europe and Sweden. Political shades of opinion did not much affect this image as yet. We meet again the obligatory idols, Washington and Franklin, and the latter has now become a national classic. There are eight Norwegian translations of *Poor Richard* down to the Civil War, eleven more after that, and three biographies, one in comic-strip form. Much attention was also paid to Lafayette, hero of three revolutions. Interest was not limited to academic circles. Long after the middle of the century, a list of Norwegian ships contains the names of Columbus, George Washington, Franklin, Lafayette, and even Leiv Eiriksson.

More important was the position of America in the tempestuous contemporary world. The Monroe Doctrine was paid notice, and even more the speeches of American statesmen against the Holy Alliance and their expressions of sympathy toward fighting Greece, Portugal, and Spain. Again the poets voiced their confidence in the free New World. The details of American life reported by the papers remained overwhelmingly positive with regard to economic progress, the legal system, popular education, and general "morality, happiness and freedom."

This worship does not mean that Norwegian readers were unacquainted with the rising wave of European criticism of America, voiced particularly in travel books. Rather, the reports were simply not believed. Several papers printed parodies ridiculing the grotesque images of America commonly found in British periodicals.

In contemporary Sweden, the dawn of Romanticism around

1820 influenced the image of America negatively. There was no such tendency in Norway. On the contrary, American creative writing now added color to the popular picture. In 1821 *Morgenbladet* (The Morning Post) printed Sidney Smith's famous article with the question: "Who ever reads an American book?" But about the same time the first translations of James Fenimore Cooper's novels arrived from Denmark and were devoured by the Norwegians. In 1835 we are told that "the works of the greatest writers, W. Scott, Cooper, Schiller, and Goethe, are read or even owned in every cultivated Norwegian home." Washington Irving made his appearance at the same time.

The general feeling of fellowship was expressed symbolically when, in 1821, Norway chose the form of its new national flag. Among the many suggested designs were several star-spangled banners. The parliamentary committee favored a design with five stars, one for each diocese. Although in the end the stars were left out, it was emphasized that at least the colors red, white, and blue were those of the other "liberty flags." When it came to the application of the American image and its tradition of ideas to Norwegian everyday life, opinions were not so uniform.

The Norwegian constitution contained the framework of a far-reaching political democracy. But social stratification remained, together with many economic privileges. Government largely remained in the hands of "the establishment," officialdom and bourgeoisie, through a cabinet appointed at will by the king. Moreover, at the very first session of Parliament, it became clear that many on the governmental side now regretted the democratic concessions granted in the constitution.

On the other side, the majority of the people, the farmers, were raising demands for a limitation of the power of bureaucracy, a more extended popular self-government, and removal of many economic restrictions. These demands had not yet crystallized into a clear political program, but a movement of opposition manifested itself almost immediately. Given the esteem felt for America by the general public, it was unavoidable that transatlantic parallels would soon present themselves.

The problem of religious liberty, pushed under the carpet at Eidsvoll, was brought up again repeatedly, not only as a matter of principle but also as a means of curtailing the power of the clergy. The government itself raised the question with regard to the Quakers, but the opposition demanded complete religious tolerance. The American vice-consul in Christiania was one of the main spokesmen of the reform, together with his brother, who had been an "ardent Jacobin" in revolutionary Paris. The bill was not passed, but discussion showed that both sides were now drawing their arguments from America.

The same dichotomy appeared in the question of nobility, an institution which had been abolished at Eidsvoll. The king tried in vain to introduce it again and was met with strong references to America. ("Franklin and Washington were no noblemen.") But a government paper pointed out that the "wealthy and well-bred" squires in the American Congress really lacked nothing of nobility but the very name. A similar cleavage appeared in the discussion of free enterprise: the nonexistence of guilds in America was praised by the opposition, while there was still skepticism on the conservative side.

Much more profound contrasts were touched upon when it came to the actual form of government. Christian Magnus Falsen now veered toward the restrictive side and again presented his 1814 version of the American Senate, with no more success. Instead, the farmers demanded the establishment of municipality boards, "similar to the American federative arrangement," a "communalism" which was going to become a main point in the opposition program.

On both sides, such arguments were still presented with polite bows across the ocean, but beneath the surface there were also more violent reactions. In 1822 an old army officer warned against the terrifying future strength of the United States and, with even more vehemence, denounced the democrats of that nation, "the most wild and bloodthirsty among political sects," who threatened their country with "a great catastrophe."

The Second Decade: Henrik Wergeland

The years from the middle 1820s to the late 1830s in many ways are a continuation of the previous period. The great world event was the July Revolution of 1830, the first wave of enthusiasm followed by new reaction. The impact was strongly felt even in Norway. However, the distinguishing mark there was the emergence into public life of a group of highly talented youngsters, who were going to mold Norway's fate for generations to come.

The overtowering figure is Henrik Wergeland (1808-1845). It is hard to explain to non-Norwegians the position he holds in his nation. He was a lyrical poet of genius; if he were translatable, he would belong to world literature. This gift was matched by his power of human sympathy and empathy: he wished to use his immense powers in the service of mankind and, above all, of his own nation. The twenty-three huge volumes of his *Collected Works* are testimony to his tireless effort to enlighten and educate his fellow-countrymen. In making that effort, he pointed to most of the tasks, political, social, and cultural, that were to dominate the strivings of his nation down to this day.

For such reasons, it became a matter of historic importance that, from the very beginning, the United States was an essential element of Wergeland's thinking about the past and, to an even greater degree, the future. America could be only one moment among many. Wergeland's world was universal in the literal sense; he moved playfully from the cosmic to the tiniest detail of existence. But characteristic of this world was its internal unity: the bloody popular risings around 1830 were just forms of the universal struggle of the spirit in all creatures. From his teen-age years onward, the United States held its place as the country of origin of his fighting gospel.

In his earliest poems, Wergeland outlined his view of history. Law-bound popular freedom had its golden age in Old Norse society and in the republics of classical antiquity. Servitude came with Caesar and lasted until the American Revolution, seed-bed of all other popular risings. After the revolution in July 1830, Wergeland exultantly greeted his heroes, Washington, Kościuszko, and Lafayette, and their victories: "every night gives birth to a morning more red." Soon, the Holy Alliance would be a somber memory. These ideas were elaborated again and again. The heroes appeared and reappeared, along with their well-known adjectives; Socrates, Washington, and Franklin had "perfected the ideal of humanity." America was "the distant foster land of our liberty." The treatment of the

Negro was a dark spot, but in the early 1830s, still the only one.

These were typically "enlightened" ideas, called to life by the imagination of a great romantic poet akin to Walt Whitman (although they were not known to each other). Wergeland delighted in the melodious American river names; he made his political heroes move under the cool shelter of acacias and sycamores. But he did not accept the romantic notion that the United States was an artificial creation, to be placed below the Middle Ages with its "monkish dark." To him, it was the free Old Norse society that was reborn organically at Eidsvoll in the spirit of America.

These were no airy speculations: they were closely related to the everyday problems of Wergeland's struggle at home. The "people" to him was no abstraction but comprised all those human beings—farmers, workmen, and "plebeian servant girls"—who needed his help. He once described himself as a young man, editing his journal *For the Labor Class* "under the portraits of Franklin and Washington." He pointed to the religious freedom of the United States: no state church and hierarchy, no "compulsion of the conscience!" He wrote warmly about the temperance movement in America and the liberal view of woman and her abilities. In particular, he advocated the reform of the prisons in accordance with American ideas. He translated a book about the problem and on his deathbed was still pondering the "Pennsylvanian System."

Neither was his attitude one of vague idealism. Again and again, Wergeland pointed out that America's liberty was behind the explosive development of its economic life and general well-being. For Americans, the result was no narrow-minded egotism but humanity, large-mindedness, and public spirit, as demonstrated in the face of great natural catastrophes. Wergeland surely knew of the less attractive sides of America, but until the rising wave of emigration there from Norway, he refused to give credence to the most negative descriptions, which were now increasingly being played up by the penny press. He warned his readers not to forget that "the rotten monarchichal system of our Old World" profited by the denigration of all republicans. What else was to be expected in a Europe where the shadow of America's grandeur now reached across the ocean and, in darkest Germany, met the shadow of Russia's pyramid?

The Clash of Voices

Henrik Wergeland was a poet and a man of vision. Among his contemporaries, the image of America was largely the same as his, but it was more sober and slowly changed character. The modest Norwegian newspapers and journals still drew most of their material from foreign sources. Thus, they were also bound to reflect the negative and sensational picture of America that increasingly spread over Europe from the late 1820s.

Until the end of the 1830s, Norwegian worship of America predominated as before and received fresh support from the July Revolution. When in 1831 the students in Christiania started a collection in order to assist the fighting Poles, the money was to be sent to Lafayette, "friend of the freedom of two worlds." The newspapers in Wergeland's circle echoed his thoughts: America represented "liberalism" and "light" as contrasted to European "absolutism" and "darkness." Others extolled the United States as the ideal medium, a homogeneous society of the middle class. It was suggested that the Norwegian Parliament send young men across the sea to study American public life.

In most fields the speed of American progress was "unbelievable," according to the newspapers. Some of these reports sound like disguised replies to rising criticism. Thus, it was reported that in Philadelphia, an immense crowd which gathered to celebrate George Washington's centenary in 1832 had displayed a calm and self-discipline that was proof of their "moral orderliness." The first large-scale American philanthropic impulse in Norway belongs to these years: the organized temperance movement heralded by Wergeland swiftly spread to "almost every parish of Southern Norway."

But besides the paeans, other tunes can now be heard, for which the most informative source is the leading daily of the time, *Morgenbladet*. Until 1848 the paper belonged to the opposition group, Wergeland's followers. Repeatedly, the editor printed descriptions of American life that can only be called paradisiac, without shadows. But gradually this material came to be intermingled with items of a totally different character, news that just couldn't be swept aside as reactionary propaganda. Obviously, everyday life in the United States also included poverty and alcoholism, violence and recklessness. The bank and monetary crises were followed carefully. Above all, American political life seemed to be far removed from "moral orderliness." Andrew Jackson struggled hard against the moneyed aristocracy at home, and Congress deserved its "detestable celebrity." As early as 1832 "civil war" was mentioned as thinkable.

The paper discussed this material as well as it was able to, trying to fit it into America's generally positive image. Thus, even in Norway we can follow that quiet process of adaptation which, among the great powers, had been going on for quite a while. The "enlightened philosophers" of the previous century had believed in a human nature of universal validity, and on this basis they had constructed an America radiant in its simplification. In small and provincial Norway, with poor and second-hand knowledge, that image was bound to become even more uncomplicated and even more persistent. Now the stereotypes began dissolving under the pressure of real America.

What particularly dawned upon people was the realization that all comparison was dangerous. In 1826 a Norwegian newspaper made the observation that the United States "does not resemble Europe in anything." Six years later, *Morgenbladet* discussed Frances Trollope's famous American travel book. The reviewer was quite critical but found the book instructive because it showed "how strangely the way of life over there differs from ours."

The application of such observations to Norwegian politics still remained scattered. The farmers' opposition made headway, and in 1833 they appeared in force in Parliament for the first time. In their press there are references to favorable American conditions and popular power, although not too often. The major victory of the farmers, the introduction of local self-government in 1837—what the Conservative Prime Minister called "a new attempt at republicanization"—largely followed European models. But in 1833 the man who would lead the farmers for more than a generation, Ole Gabriel Ueland (1799-1870), took his seat in Parliament. Although he had had a poor schooling, he was an assiduous reader, and America became one of his permanent interests. He made a brilliant debut with a speech during a debate on tariffs, flailing his adversary with American parallels.

On the Conservative side, the attitude was more hesitant. Yet even here a kind of front now slowly developed: the people "of principle and property" joined forces against new threats. The leaders called themselves "the intelligentsia" and from 1830 to 1832 published the journal *Vidar*. Their guiding spirit was the future leader of the government party, the brilliant jurist A. M. Schweigaard (1808-1870). These men were moderate reformers, not reactionaries in the continental sense. But they were disturbed by "the demagogical element" in the constitution and hated revolutionary liberalism with its Roman-French-American pathos.

Their journal reflected such ideas, even with respect to America. Sometimes the reporting was neutral and sober. Other times even the images of the saints were touched upon irreverently: George Washington himself had had to obey "the dictatorship of the mob." The journal printed an article about social life in North America which repeated all the worst British allegations and added a similar condemnation of American "hardheartedness," "dollar-worship," lack of justice, economic exploitation, and "general atmosphere of trickery."

The leading poet of the group, J. S. Welhaven (1807-1873), spoke his mind no less clearly. He was a libertarian in theory and admired the youthfulness of the New World, but so far as conditions in contemporary Norway were concerned, he found the declamations of Thomas Paine and Marat to be idle talk.

From 1836 the government group had its own daily. It, too, published a good deal of sober reporting, but there were also shocked references to the results of "leaving most of the sovereign rights in the hands of the riffraff," as was the case in the United States. There seemed to be a growing doubt among Americans themselves about "the metaphysical foundation" of the constitution. Surely, their democracy and their money seemed to keep a kind of equilibrium. But that balance offered a problematic comfort.

American Becomes Real, 1837-1861

The historic turning point in relations between Norway and the United States was the period beginning in the late 1830s.

Until then, transatlantic contacts had not only been sparse but had had a touch of the abstract. Still, Norway itself was largely isolated from the economic and social powers that were transforming the world in general. The country was poor, its agriculture static, its industry an enlarged handicraft, and its shipping limited to European waters. Norwegians read about America in the newspapers, but they often had no real frame of reference. But from the late 1830s a development began which, in the course of a few decades, was going to pull Norway into the mainstream of industrial capitalism and increasingly make the two countries follow the same track.

By the 1840s Norway's relation to Sweden receded into the background for a while. Interest became focused on internal economic growth, which was increasingly guided by liberalistic principles; Norway entered "the period of the stomach." Communications developed fast, and agriculture modernized its methods. But other occupations now gained precedence. City population was doubled between 1835 and 1865. The old barter economy was on its way out. Banks facilitated the circulation of money; industry and, from the 1850s, shipping on the seven seas gained a new importance. Expansion was accompanied by a new sense of national identity.

However, new tensions developed simultaneously, above all because of a rapid increase of population, which was growing faster at that time in Norway than in any other European country. The number of Norwegians doubled between 1815 and 1865. The result was a continuous population pressure which was made even more acute by an international economic crisis. In the year of revolution, 1848, the social agitator Marcus Thrane (1817-1890) was the first Norwegian to raise radical demands on behalf of the underprivileged. His popular support was such that in 1851, the frightened authorities put the movement down by force. During this period of growth, turbulence, and change in Norway, America came to play a completely new part.

At first, population movement occurred within Norway itself, as people sought a livelihood in other regions and in the cities. America was still beyond the horizon. But in 1817 a shipwrecked Dutchman came into the port of Bergen with 500 German emigrants on their way to the United States. The incident was much talked of everywhere, and fantastic rumors followed. In 1821 the first explorer was sent across the Atlantic to investigate possibilities, and in 1825 the sloop *Restauration* left for America with a load of 52 emigrants. There followed an interval of a decade, until in 1836 almost 200 left. They were the beginning of an avalanche.

The movement soon spread all over the country south of the Polar Circle, town and countryside alike. Its explosive character is an indication of the accumulated social tension peculiar to Norway at the time. In Denmark and Sweden, the movement did not get under way until the 1850s and never reached the same proportions. Everywhere the pattern was similar. The most important direct impulse came from the emigrants themselves. Their letters soon reached Norway by the thousands, were copied and circulated, and often printed in the papers. They aroused a tremendous debate and, above all, stimulated the desire to leave. Even more influential were emigrants on visits home; they often organized a new exodus and also paid for the tickets. In 1838 came the first book of emigration propaganda, by the famous Ole Rynning (1809-1838), and others followed.

The movement was often called epidemic, and properly so. In 1843 the number of emigrants was 1,600; around 1850 the annual average was 3,600, and in the year 1861 the number reached 8,850. The total figure for the period 1825-1865 was 78,000. This was just a modest beginning, compared with the postbellum years. But the effect must have been shocking to a nation whose capital in 1855 had only 30,000 inhabitants.

Thus, in the course of a few years, emigration created a transatlantic connection which completely overshadowed all previous contacts. The movement of population soon became part of a much more extensive interplay in the economic field. The United States still was in need of tremendous imports; during this period, Norway sent more than half of its production of iron there. Emigrant ships played a part in such trade; they frequently also took a load of iron or other European goods, and on their way back carried tobacco, cotton, and rice to Norway, or lumber from Canada to England. The Norwegian merchant marine grew more rapidly at this time than those of other nations, largely because of the traffic to and from America. In 1854 Norwegian emigrant ships to Canada outnumbered those of all other countries.

At the same time, American technical know-how began making its influence felt, particularly after the first World Exhibition, held in London in 1851, which displayed sensational American machines. Norwegian journals printed numerous articles with illustrations, above all of the new agricultural implements. Models were distributed to farmers and were swiftly imitated. There were similar American improvements in navigation (e.g., M. F. Maury's calendar). The main innovation was an American clipper ship with a long and sharp hull, made for fast sailing. Norwegians began building such ships in the 1850s, and soon they were to be seen on all oceans.

"A Scandal Among the Nations"

Not all aspects of the intensive and many-sided contact between Norwegians and Americans need to be given equal consideration in this book. Norwegians settled in relatively few of the American states. They stuck together and maintained many of their national characteristics for several generations. The "Norwegian America" thus created is an interesting phenomenon, and in recent years its development has been investigated with great care. But from the very beginning, most of the Norwegians who emigrated to America were destined to become assimilated and lost to the nation of their birth. In this book, their fate can be of interest only as far as it influenced their homeland. Splendid research has lately been devoted to emigration itself as a social process. Here, we can be concerned only with the aspects typical of emigration to the United States.

In this matter, purely psychological factors are of a high order. Up to the 1840s, America had existed, as far as Norway is concerned, mainly as an image in the minds of a few individuals, largely of the educated class. Overnight, the country now became close and factual, a part of everyday life, to an increasing number of ordinary people. Many general social factors were at play in this connection. But at bottom were always the ideas and decisions of individual human beings and that image of America on which they were founded. Thus, it was of decisive importance that, due to emigration, the very flow of information about America now became more extensive and varied.

In Norway, as in most European nations, academic studies of America were still rare. The Greek, Latin, and German languages dominated the University of Christiania, while English was rather regarded with contempt. But other fields were better off. From 1850 to 1859, A. M. Schweigaard gave four university courses in American "statistics," which at that time meant a mixture of history, political geography, and political science. In the secondary schools, English was made a voluntary subject from the 1850s onward, and some attention was also paid to America. In 1873 "The World Importance of the American War of Independence" was set as a paper for the countrywide final examination.

Much more important was the increase of popular information. A surprising number of "periodical publications" were started in Norway in the antebellum years, and many of them reveled in the reports on America carried by the foreign press. Thus, they became instrumental in the distribution of the new, realistic image of America, and in particular of those small, colorful, and often grotesque glimpses of American life—now frequently accompanied by illustrations—which were often more influential than any serious article.

An analysis has been made of Americana in the two most widely circulated Norwegian weeklies of the time (1835-1866), one more popular, the other more sophisticated. In both, the quantity is surprisingly large. Even more significant is the disjointed character of the material, a jumble of facts and curios, congressional elections and camp meetings, lynchings and buffalo hunts, household remedies and Jenny Lind. This external mess reflects a resigned intellectual confusion: there was no longer a general image of America; that strange country was so motley and self-contradictory.

In addition to the appeal to popular taste, there was also, both in the weekly and in the daily press, a definite growth in the amount of competent information. A number of Norwegian journalists and academic writers now began specializing in foreign affairs and were well-informed even on American problems.

The new economic contacts also for the first time took a number of Norwegians to the United States every year as part of their jobs. But the most important new sources of information were the emigrants and their letters, circulated or printed. Their field of vision often was narrow, but they also were bound to tell a good deal about American conditions generally. Again there was a mixture of black and white. The emigrants' accounts are remarkable for their expression of personal experience and their personal intimacy. Very often the writers addressed themselves to their own native districts and to the lower classes to which they themselves belonged. And they communicated their news outside the official channels. Soon, Norwegian-American papers also appeared in the homeland, presenting the new country as seen from the grass-roots.

The new image of America emerging from these manifold sources did not appear in a void. It was also molded by the Norwegian contemporary background and its actual needs. Here there are conflicting forces. In part, the material is meager and has not yet been investigated. But again, emigration is at the center.

Until the 1850s, it was commonly accepted that the emigration that was then beginning was disastrous to the country and a pure loss. Equally general was the idea that the government should not in any way interfere with the economic forces at work. Almost twenty years were needed before even some simple regulations protecting the emigrants against the hardships of the crossing were passed. But this apparent agreement covered highly divergent opinions, some of them about America itself.

Emigration was bound to call for strong reactions, not least on the government side. Like most administrations, the conservative Norwegian bureaucracy, from the cabinet down, was quite well pleased with its performance. But emigration sprang from a discontent with conditions in Norway, which were driving people away; complaints soon became numerous and vocal. The government well knew that these reactions formed part of that general opposition which had long extolled the United States as its great ideal. Thus, it became good government policy to point out the negative sides of America: it was a risky place for immigrants, and democracy held many dangers and had many flaws.

The government also had its own channels of information. The Swedish-appointed diplomats in Washington, D.C., mostly felt their position as a banishment and had no love for the American political system. The few Norwegians who now gradually were admitted to diplomatic service did not feel differently.

The government distributed some of this negative information, but largely contented itself with the writings against emigration by individual officials, beginning as early as 1837 with a pastoral letter from a bishop. Charles Dickens's skeptical *American Notes* appeared in Norwegian translation in 1843, and the government paper praised it as "no more flattering than Tocqueville's book." The same year also saw the publication of the first (and only) fascicle of Dickens's *Martin Chuzzlewit,* his most anti-American novel.

Even more important was the papers' constant injection of American news items fitting into the conservative image. Often, such material was presented in grotesque and complacent detail and with a note of fun and flippancy that was going to remain. But there was a consistent thought behind it; many times it just reflected the pessimistic views of contemporary Americans. The decline of America was striking, the papers reported, even during the short time since the appearance of Tocqueville's book. American home politics were not only primitive and vulgar but corrupt, and ever more dominated by vested interests. The messy population was represented by unprincipled politicians, the judicial system unreliable, economic life dishonest, religion grotesque, and intellectual activity flat and insipid. The "Wild West" had lost its romantic attraction. The king of humbug, P. T. Barnum, now justly represented his nation to the world. America had betrayed even its international task: American behavior toward Mexico was only too familiar.

Similar ideas, not necessarily borrowed from abroad, were expressed in the remarkable posthumous "views of his time" of the young jurist L. Th. Barner (1819-1853). He was a moderate conservative who hated the France of Louis Napoleon and loved England. In comparison, the American republic to him had failed, making power "the spoil of victory" and leaving leadership in the hands of mediocrity. The matchless economic advantages of the country might still disguise the fact that the population itself no longer was marked by that "humanity and respect for human rights" that were the prerequisites of real freedom. The enthusiasts were in for disappointment.

The change of opinion is particularly striking in some of the old liberals. The historian L. Kr. Daa (1809-1877), a friend of the young Wergeland, in his early years frequently referred to America in his battles for good causes. But he was rather a moderate liberal of the English type and loved political liberty more than social equality. The events of 1848 disturbed him and even influenced his view of

America. Tocqueville had taught him that democracy might lead to a tyranny by the masses. In the 1850s Daa saw that tendency prevailing in the United States, and the country veering toward oligarchy. In the end, he condemned the American Constitution itself. The republic which the Europeans so long had regarded as perfect "now is very close to being judged a scandal among the nations."

Even foreigners noticed the shift of opinion. The famous American philanthropist Charles L. Brace visited Norway twice, in 1851 and 1856. The first time, he found America to be the ideal of liberal Norwegians in all classes of society, even to the point of exaggeration. By the time of his second visit, the turn-about was complete: the Americans were regarded as semi-barbarians, unreliable and brutal, equipped with the worst vices of the Old World but with none of its refinement.

Among creative writers, emigration now made its appearance as an important subject. Some of them were only playing on the emotions involved. Others warned against leaving Norway but said little about America itself; they praised the good old country or painted the painful farewell and the unavoidable nostalgia. But disparagement of the new homeland also crept in easily: emigrants' dreams were not being fulfilled. Some writers belonged on the side of the opposition: the real tasks awaited at home.

The outstanding example of this changing atmosphere is no less than Henrik Wergeland himself. The turning point in his relation to America is the first great emigration year 1836-1837. He did not condemn emigration in principle; sometimes even he himself toyed with the idea of leaving. But the fact that free farmers in his own Norway could do such a thing ran against all his ideas: it was "an unbelievable rage" and a "national disaster," and he would do anything to stop it.

This decision did not dim his judgment. He continued pointing to the conditions at home which made people emigrate. But things could be changed and new livelihoods opened if energies were directed toward the tasks in Norway itself: there is fish in the ocean, and unbroken soil in the North! He soon discovered that such admonitions were of no avail, however. Unavoidably, he was thus driven toward that general denigration of America which was typical of his political adversaries.

He began by criticizing details, such as the common bond-service of immigrants in return for prepaid tickets. But in the 1840s even the general picture turned darker. In his journal *For the Labor Class,* Wergeland translated in 1843—obviously with approval—a German article which not only pointed out American callousness toward newcomers, unbelievably hard work, mortgages, and foreclosures, but also made more sweeping assertions about the "impotence of the government" and the "complete lack of sincerity." Wergeland could mention as a well-known fact that the "egotistic Yankees" have "a dollar where other people have their hearts." His last literary work, written on his deathbed, was a play warning against emigration: the agents do not tell the truth!

Although Wergeland did not give up the basic enthusiasm which characterized the generation of 1814, he never tried to work the new contrasts into a consistent image. Even in this he was prophetic, giving voice to the unsolved conflict, which remains to this day, between the traditions of the American past, heralded by Wergeland in his youth, and the new economic and social developments which pointed elsewhere.

Similar features are prominent in the case of young Björnstjerne Björnson (1832-1910). He became Wergeland's successor and, like him, held a position in his nation's life rarely equaled by writers in other countries. He was a poet, playwright, and novelist of the first rank and in 1903 was awarded the Nobel prize for literature. Like Wergeland, he used most of his immense powers in the service of his fellow beings. He was the leading Norwegian orator of his time, a stupendous writer of articles and pamphlets, and the author of 30,000 letters. He threw himself with dynamic force into the political, social, and literary battles of his country with an enthusiasm and power of conviction that made him the most beloved and most hated Norwegian of his age.

It was to be of historic importance that a man of such dimensions was absorbed in America from his early youth on. Perhaps the first book Björnson bought with money he had earned himself was one by Emerson. But initially, emigration disturbed him as it did Wergeland. His brilliant early pictures from Norwegian farm life are quiet appeals to remain at home.

Björnson was even more disturbed by the unpleasant features, well-known by now, of American contemporary life. The newspaper which he edited from 1856 to 1858 has almost nothing but negative reports from the United States, that "febrile" place where "everything and everybody are whirled off by steam to Heaven or Hell." He saw with horror the same materialism gaining ground in Norway with the growth of industry: Christiania was becoming "an American frontier town" where the tender growth was being "thundered down" by the incessant din of material interests.

Equality and Prosperity

When it came to stemming the tide of emigration, however, all these frightening descriptions proved to be almost without effect, and one may fairly question their reach and real importance. Within the broad population of Norwegians, there remained the conviction which Goethe had put into words when he cried: "America, you are better off!" And this conviction had its own arguments.

One of the first emigrants, Gjert G. Hovland, who left Norway in 1831, was also a great writer of letters home. Almost right away they gained a wide circulation and were read avidly. His list of good things in the new country strikingly characterized its popular attraction and made much of the criticism of the literati sound bookish and overly sophisticated. America had an abundance of land, wrote Hovland, fertile and cheap. There was no expensive bureaucracy, and taxes were hardly worth mentioning. The common man had the same political and legislative power as the well-to-do, and he made the laws for his own good. There were complete social equality, full liberty of thought, religion, and occupation, "plenty of space for everybody, and flowering prosperity almost everywhere."

This list, of course, also reflects the negative conditions at home which made people susceptible to the allurements of America and suspicious toward the official warnings. There was a general feeling that in Norway, "liberty" actually did not mean much to the common man. The totally different attitude of Americans whetted his criticism, raised his demands, aroused "strange longings," and strengthened his courage to break away.

By itself, this image of the United States was bound to be helpful to the political opposition. Farm leaders had always regarded emigration as a perfectly legitimate social phenomenon. One of them, Hans Barlien, a radical and an inveterate reader of Voltaire, after his emigration in 1838 wrote home that "for the first time I now can breathe freely." Ole Rynning, on his departure to America in 1837, wrote aboard ship the first "Norwegian-American" poem, which recalled the old-time voyage of Leiv Eiriksson to "Vinland the Good." But the real aim of both Barlien and Rynning was to help the laboring class at home in their battle against the establishment. Others saw emigration in a large historical perspective, as a movement of "a moral and material grandeur unequalled in human history."

The attacks of those who were critical of America were not left unanswered. Indirectly, Ole Rynning's book was a reply to them, and eager journalists soon started violent polemics in the same vein. Most effective, however, was the quiet and ceaseless flow of emigrants' letters to the newspapers; the bulk of them told simply and straightforwardly of the good life over there. Around 1850 there even existed in Chicago a club of Norwegians writing circular letters in order to tell people in Norway about the "equality and spirit of liberty" typical of the American nation. These letters largely described a rural America that was fast becoming less typical. But this hindsight on our part does not affect the truthfulness of the letter-writers and their tremendous impact.

Moreover, all through the period, these reports from the frontier were supplemented by material which gave a positive picture of America as a whole. There was a realization, not limited to the opposition press, that British travelers were unreliable witnesses. Friendly descriptions from all runs of American life appeared in quantity even in the conservative papers. They could appeal to a continued interest, not only in American history, but also in the many colorful and spectacular contemporary aspects of the western wonderland. Curiosity was satisfied by a broadly popular literature of information about America which now made its appearance.

In much of this writing, there was also a developing shift of emphasis. America of the past with its progressive political ideologies was being insensibly overshadowed by modern America with its progress in technique and economy and its unbelievable practical prospects, a "youthful" nation in a different meaning of the word. Even then, this America was felt as an admonition in a new sense. Its impact was going to grow in strength with Norway's own industrialization and capitalization: the Americans could teach the Norwegians to use their own resources as *they* did! Their "materialism" surely was much to be preferred to Old World "sluggishness and negligence."

Most of the emigrants' letters naturally told about daily drudgery which only gradually created a tolerable comfort. Yet the conviction never disappeared that America was the fairyland where everything might happen. The returning emigrant often offered visible testimony. He made an impression not only by his lack of subservience toward bailiffs and ministers but quite as much by his clothing, his watch chain, and billfold. Soon there came success stories of an even more surprising kind, and they were duly publicized.

The amazing confirmation of this material side of the American dream was, of course, the California gold rush beginning in 1854. Norwegian diggings were relatively modest, but the impact on the imagination was immense: the entire continent seemed to appear through a golden haze.

The depth of such emotions was demonstrated in a curious way in the life story of the violin virtuoso Ole Bull (1810-1880). He was the first Norwegian to win world fame. At the same time, he was a fervent patriot, a friend of Henrik Wergeland, and an America enthusiast in the old style. He toured the United States five times with resounding success, composed tone poems to Niagara Falls and to the memory of George Washington, married an American woman, and spent his last ten years in her homeland.

In 1851 Bull decided to found in Pennsylvania a Norwegian colony named Oleana, "dedicated to Liberty." He took out American citizenship at a ceremony in Independence Hall in Philadelphia, delivering on that occasion a lofty speech on American conditions compared with those at home. Although his plans for the settlement were exciting, he was swindled by speculators, and the undertaking collapsed almost right away. The most lasting result was an amusing song ridiculing the fantastic popular dreams of Ole Bull's American paradise where the Norwegian slave is knighted, roasted pigs serve themselves, and the brooks are running with beer. The sarcastic attitude of this song was, however, not typical of the general feeling about America.

Sobering Judgment

In the 1850s in particular, the trend of development was toward a more varied and objective view of the United States.

In the first place, this holds true of emigration itself. There was still propaganda against it, but gradually the note became less hysterical. The phenomenon was accepted more and more as inevitable. Economic progress proved that the population movement was not leading to catastrophe. Even Norwegian officials had to admit that emigrants willing to work normally found acceptable living conditions across the ocean. A Norwegian paper wrote in 1861 that the denigration of America was now a waste of time: most of those who had left were "quite well informed."

Even in the general image of America during this period one may perhaps perceive a growing balance and consolidation. There was a striking decrease in the quantity of American items in the public media. The change was hardly due to the more interesting news about the Crimean War. It seems more probable that readers were tiring a little of the endless sensationalism of articles about America.

One factor of importance in this shift may be that, because of new and swiftly developing contacts between the two countries, America presented itself to Norwegians in many more contexts than before and often in an extremely positive way. American goods and artifacts were still rare, but there was an importation of new ideas, no longer just political, but humanitarian and cultural also.

In the old question of prison reform, an impressive new penitentiary planned by the government was finally finished in Christiania in 1851. Everybody knew that both of the two opposing principles for its construction were American.

In the alcohol question, from the late 1840s the early temperance movement was swiftly replaced by the movement for abstinence (in the beginning just from hard liquor). That idea too had roots in the United States and was strongly furthered in Norway by an American Methodist preacher, R. Baird. There was probably also an American impulse behind the total prohibition of distillation of alcohol which was passed by the Parliament in 1842, but not sanctioned by the government.

The success which American women had achieved in gaining greater rights and opportunities for themselves became known in Norway in the 1850s through a book by the famous Swedish author Fredrika Bremer. She was an inspiration to Henrik Wergeland's sister, Camilla Collett (1813-1895), when in 1855 she was the first to champion feminism in earnest on Norwegian soil. American developments in the field were often regarded with suspicion, but reports began crossing the ocean both about the impressive cultural activity of American women and about their admission to academic studies, which occurred there much earlier than in Norway.

The peace movement similarly reached the country from the United States during these decades, particularly when Elihu Burritt, the famous "learned blacksmith from Connecticut," became the motive power behind it. Burritt's monthly peace articles appeared in Norwegian papers, and there were Norwegian delegates at the international peace conferences.

Religious movements made the strongest impact, however. Religious life was strong among the Norwegians on the new soil from the very beginning. But the state church at home soon started organizing the American congregations; by 1860 most of the immigrant Norwegians had joined the Norwegian-American Lutheran church, which maintained contact with the homeland and served as an important link of communication.

The most sensational, and also most original, religious creation of the New World, Mormonism, developed in opposition to Lutheranism. Norwegians early joined Joseph Smith. The first Mormon emissary went to Norway in 1857, and missionary work has gone on ever since. But violent attacks were directed against Mormonism, and the sect has made little headway in Norway as compared to Denmark and Sweden.

The really important impact came from American religious movements which were less exotic and thus could make their influence felt upon the Lutheran church in the homeland. The Methodist and Baptist churches, in their organized forms, spread to Norway from the United States in 1853 and 1857, respectively. They both proved to have great missionary power and were in close contact with their American headquarters. They both became factors to be reckoned with after the American Civil War.

American universities were still quite undeveloped, and academic contacts across the ocean were few, with the exception of the first exchanges of books organized by the Smithsonian Institution. Norwegian medical men visited America and were impressed by what they saw in their field. The American invention of anesthesia was adopted in Norway right away, and Norwegian research on leprosy was applied early in Norwegian settlements in the United States.

American contemporary painting of landscape and folk life would have interested the Norwegians of the time, who in a similar way were struggling for a national identity. But the field still was largely unknown outside America. So was musical life. Even in belles lettres, very few Norwegians as yet seem to have read the great American writers of the period. Some of them, of course, would not be recognized for a long time even in their homeland. But Norwegian newspapers at the middle of the century occasionally began picking up items about recent American books and writers from the foreign press, making at least some of the leading names known.

When it came to the translation of foreign works, Norway was in a special situation. During the period of union, Danish had been introduced as the official language. While work was now under way to make Norwegian prevail even in the written idiom, foreign literature was still read mainly in Danish translations. But in the early 1850s the first serious effort was made to go directly to the sources. Harriet Beecher Stowe's world success, *Uncle Tom's Cabin,* paved the way (1853). It was followed by her *Mayflower,* and—more important—by Hawthorne's *The Scarlet Letter* (1855). The lighter genre was introduced by the sentimental and immensely popular Susan Warner.

In the great nations on the European continent, disillusionment about America set in with a vengeance in the decades before the Civil War, often in sweeping generalizations. In comparison, Norwegian opinion is hard to gauge. But the slender material seems to indicate that negativism was less marked in Norway than in France, for instance, and that the positive image of the previous generation better held its ground.

One reason surely was the time-lag natural in a small and marginal nation. The traditions of the eighteenth century still were deeply rooted in Norway. Also, political conservatism was quite moderate compared to its foreign counterparts. But the main reason doubtless was that feeling of fellowship which had been so keen when the nation gained its independence and which in the following years was given additional strength by a personality as overpowering as that of Henrik Wergeland. In few nations of Europe did the United States come to be tied to national traditions and to broad popular movements to the same extent, and to create such genuine enthusiasm. Emigration appears as a natural continuation of this development.

Taken altogether, even the day-to-day reportage in the Norwegian press about the United States before the Civil War perhaps may also be characterized as relatively balanced. The impression is confirmed by more general evalutions of America. They occurred even in the dailies, which then resembled serious periodicals more than newspapers. *Morgenbladet* in the 1850s translated a long series of sober and competent articles about American society which were written by well-known foreign experts, such as the British Lord Carlisle and the Frenchmen A. Cucheval-Clarigny and Philarète Chasles. A similar series of thirty articles in the same paper was anonymous and thus may well have been written by a Norwegian author. There were many briefer articles of a similar kind.

Books on America were still rare and were usually unpretentious compilations in history and geography aimed at a general audience. But, on the whole, they were not polemical. Even Ole Rynning's propaganda for emigration has been praised by American historians for its acumen and calm judgment. L. Th. Barner's skeptical assessment ended up by pointing to America's "unparalleled" progress. England was on its way out; "the next period of civilization is going to be American."

The most weighty Norwegian contribution to American studies in the nineteenth century was a three-volume work, almost 2,000 pages in length, about the jury system in Great Britain, Canada, and the United States which was published in 1850-1852 by the civil servant Ole Munch Ræder. Both in this book and in his printed letters from his American sojourn, Ræder appeared as a moderate conservative. But he was objective in the extreme. He held American democracy in high regard: to him, hardly any nation in history had succeeded so well in combining "liberty, order, and popular happiness."

The work of Alexis de Tocqueville was never translated into Norwegian, as it was into Swedish, but it was well known and was judged soberly. When Tocqueville died in 1859, two young law students, later to become leading Conservatives, published a long necrology of "this wonderful man" with his healthy moderation. America was the victim of "conflicting prejudices" and was described by the British with "malicious distortion." But Tocqueville understood the nation against its special background, as a result of general forces. The authors shared Tocqueville's concern lest equality and despotism join hands, but they did not use him as a conservative arsenal. Rather, they saw some of the envisaged dangers as imaginary.

These were judgments of academic learning. To the broad population, America was a personal matter in a more direct sense. Therefore, the concluding figure of this chapter should be the journalist, humorist, and lyrical poet A. O. Vinje (1818-1870). He, too, had an academic training and a cultural breadth of vision rarely equaled among his contemporaries. But he was a cotter's son and never forgot his home region and its people. He approached the everyday problems of his nation with a fearless realism which made his writings one of the great intellectual stimulations of his generation.

Vinje met the American dream in his boyhood in the valley, knew physically the hardships that turned people into emigrants, and found it to be a sensible thing to leave the country as they did. At the same time, he judged with a cool eye the life that the immigrants faced after their arrival. In his journalism in the 1850s, he pointed to all of the seamy sides of contemporary America. He also clearly saw the real range of the problem: mankind plays for high stakes over there; "all the maxims about liberty are being put to the test." But up to the Civil War, his faith in progress prevailed. In America, the tenet of the new liberalism was made a reality: "Everyone and everything are left to themselves!" The immensity of the forces at work made Vinje believe that "all is going to end well."

In 1852 a huge American panorama of the Mississippi, a precursor of our movies, was showed in Christiania. In his review Vinje "gave himself over to his illusory nature." He vividly imagined the savagery, recklessness, and brutal contrasts of the frontier in its delirious excess of power, "like the genius awakening to consciousness." But equally well he saw the romantic allurement, in nature as in life, the boundless exuberance, and the unbelievable promises: "the air of America is warm." In the previous year Henry Thoreau had seen the same panorama in the United States and had written with fascination: "I felt that this was the heroic age itself." Vinje's experience was similar.

This image was tied in with his own childhood dreams. "The future grandeur of that country stirred our self-respect, and somehow communicated to us something of its own hopes of might and power." The next generation was going to sense the full impact of that summons: "See here your heritage! All these plains belong to you. They are just waiting for human beings in order to make them happy."

Arsenal to Everyone

In many ways this antebellum period was just an overture. The forces of the future were not yet fully released. Even emigration was only in its beginnings.

Nevertheless, more than ever before America now made itself felt in the machinery of political decision. The contrasts of ideas and groups were not yet clear; the great alignments belong to the 1860s and 1870s. In most connections America was still distant and irrelevant. But references to America came to the minds of political actors more and more readily, with their general background of old stereotypes. They were used purposefully, and even here there was a certain balance: only rarely was America pointed to simply as a bugbear.

Parliament, of course, was the center of political activity. There were also other forces which considered nonparliamentary means of action. But small and rural Norway was not yet ready for social radicalism.

The year 1849 saw the arrival in Christiania of an international agitator of revolution, Harro Harring (1798-1870), a messenger from a world of more violent conflicts. He immediately joined Marcus Thrane in his battle for "the rights of the suffering classes." Harring had himself been to the United States, had no illusions, and did not encourage emigration. But compared with suppressed Europe and the fakery of Norwegian democracy, the American republic to him represented "healthy common sense." In his farce *The American Bequest,* he contrasted the international movement for freedom based on American ideas and the servility of Norwegian officialdom, and also included a quip about royalty. The government promptly shipped Harring to Denmark, and only his American citizenship and the intervention of the American vice-consul in Christiania saved him from being passed on to the Russians and certain death. His banishment aroused vigorous protests, and Parliament passed a resolution of disapproval. But none of the speakers defended Harring's ideas, let alone his American republicanism.

Harring was a stranger without contacts and actually harmless. Marcus Thrane, with his organized mass movement of indignant workers, was a different matter. He was himself fascinated by the western wonders. His newspaper strongly exhorted its readers to leave miserable Norway for the American riches. Nobody defended Ole Bull's colonization more sharply against "the slander of the well-to-do." But actually, Thrane's social ideology had little connection with the American republic. His revolutionary threats were premature, and were not backed by real force. His newspaper surely nourished the American dream in its numerous readers, but social unrest at home subsided during the years after he himself had left for America. Only indirectly, and several decades later, was the United States to become an important force in the Norwegian labor movement.

Parliament thus remained the real forum of decision. In that assembly, however, were men for whom the United States carried more far-reaching implications.

Farm leader O. G. Ueland had not forgotten his American interests, and emigration in his nearest surroundings kept them awake. But he largely was concerned with the narrow benefits of his own class. A younger leader of the group, Sören Jaabæk (1814-1894, in Parliament from 1845), had a wider outlook. He, too, was self-taught, but his range of knowledge was amazing; in later years he published a good-sized history of England. America was his elected country; he was a convinced republican of the "enlightened" type and a reader of American poetry. But he too saw most problems with the eye of the small farmer.

Very different was Johan Sverdrup (1816-1892, in Parliament from 1851), the coming leader of the Left or Liberal party and the dominant statesman of the younger generation. He was reared in the Wergeland tradition by his enthusiastic aunt, to whom Demosthenes, Washington, and Garibaldi topped the list of great citizens. Sverdrup became a politician of ideas, and America embodied the best of them. He formulated a broad democratic program inspired by Francis Lieber, among others, and based on a people educated by local self-government and participation on juries.

Sverdrup's great Conservative adversary, A. M. Schweigaard, from his youth was well grounded in things American. At his spectacular law examination, he was examined in the United States constitution. He knew the writings of Tocqueville and even taught American studies in the university, as we saw. But he hated the intellectual constructions of "natural law." He was a cautious reformer and man of the middle road, equally averse to despotism and universal suffrage. He loved England for its organic growth and was correspondingly cool toward the United States.

Foreign policy and diplomatic relations still played a minor part in the political process. All through the period of union, the Swedes largely took care of such matters; moreover, connections with the United States raised no real problems. The only context in which America was sometimes referred to was the interrelationship of the Nordic nations. A movement of "Scandinavism" advocated a strong union of these powers, partly as a protection against Russia. From the time of Henrik Wergeland onward, the federal arrangement of the United States was held up as a model in this regard. But the movement never gained ground in practical politics and in the 1860s quietly died.

The central problem, which was going to grow in importance all through the nineteenth century and dominate Norwegian political life until the dissolution of the union with Sweden in 1905, was the question of popular power. As social and economic class differences became increasingly noticeable, the propertied classes of Norway more and more closed their ranks around the cabinet. Its members were still the personal appointees of the king, and he, being a Swede, would always be marked by the conservative traditions of that nation. The opposition groups gradually rallied around a program summarized by Johan Sverdrup in one of his great speeches in Parliament: "All power gathered in this hall!" They intended to implement such ideas by pruning the actual power of king and government, above all by the introduction of "parliamentarism," making the cabinet not the servant of royalty but a reflection of the majority of the elected body representing the people.

It was not until the 1870s that such ideas were formulated clearly, although preliminary skirmishes occurred even in the period before the American Civil War. A debate of principle early touched upon a central point, the suspensive veto established by the Norwegian constitution in accordance with American practice. The government group would have preferred an absolute veto. The opposition saw in the suspensive-veto clause their only way of pressuring the government, if need be.

In 1845 A. M. Schweigaard made the contrast clear, with America as his example. Those who, in his words, would like to "make the Norwegian constitution as republican as possible" always pointed to the importance of the suspensive veto in the United States. But there was the basic difference, already underlined by Christian Magnus Falsen, that Norway had nothing corresponding to the American Senate, with its character of a conservative guarantee. Under the Norwegian system, the royal veto therefore was needed as a check in a different way. Opposition leader Ueland briefly rejected the parallel: the suspensive character of the veto to him was the vital principle of the Norwegian constitution.

Even more important was the proposal that cabinet members henceforth should be admitted to Parliament and thus implicitly become responsible to that body, not to the king. Here, of course, the Norwegian constitution closely paralleled American practice, which was praised for quite different reasons. The Conservatives naturally had no objection to this part of the American system and so were opposed to such a change. The farmers feared the presence in Parliament of the cabinet members with their superior political training and therefore were also opposed.

It was Sverdrup, the great admirer of America, who finally switched to support the proposal, thus clearing the ground for the battle in the following decades. In 1860 he declared that on this point, the fathers of the American constitution had been misled by theories and had shown considerable "political naïveté"; the mistake was now being realized even in America.

Closer to immediate interests was economic policy. Here, preliminary studies are sadly lacking, but the main trend is clear.

With growth of liberal theory, even in Norway the United States increasingly appeared as a model of "free enterprise," at least within its own borders. Sometimes there are Norwegian references to American economists, such as H. C. Carey, but more frequently to American legislation and practical measures, so different from traditional restrictive policies in Europe. On this point, government and opposition largely saw eye to eye. In the next generation, the "social problem" in our sense was going to disturb the idyll. But as yet, the sole concern of everybody was to make Norway benefit as much as possible from the conditions of a new economic world. To some extent, the United States also formed part of this game, both in regard to shipping policies and tariffs. But these details have not yet been investigated. It is probable that the American influence as yet was relatively limited.

On a number of minor points along the same line, the example of the United States sometimes came in handy. Mostly it was a question of easing and modifying the traditional Norwegian system of bureaucracy, reducing administrative fees, lightening the pressure on debtors, and generally leaving more decisions to the people. Better conditions in America could here be mentioned effectively, with emigration as a constant threat in the background. The New World, in Ueland's words, was the master of the Old "in these things as in so many others." In the fight for three important reforms, the example and experience of America were of great importance.

By an old statute of 1741, the Norwegian clergy was authorized to control lay preaching, and the law had been used ruthlessly to keep down popular religious sects. The government vetoed all modifying bills and in 1840 presented to Parliament a revised and even more restrictive version of the statute. In the arguments in favor of this bill, the United States was used as the great and terrifying example of the consequences of religious freedom. The battle against the proposal was opened by Henrik Wergeland himself, seconded by L. K. Daa. The latter referred to Tocqueville in his warm description not only of American religious life based on voluntary popular support, but of the general "public morality" of the nation. Parliament unanimously voted down both the old statute and its new version, and the decision was accepted by the government.

Another aspect of the same problem was concerned with the position of the Jews, who in the 1814 constitution had been denied access to the country. Henrik Wergeland suggested that the paragraph excluding them be eliminated, and six years after his death the proposal was passed. In his tireless fight for the reform, America was the obvious example, but it was also used by the opposite side. The Prime Minister even suggested that the introduction of a republic might be the next step. The decision was sanctioned, however. In 1845 an additional law was passed regulating the rights of other religious sects. Even in that discussion, the United States was used equally by both parties.

The second great question of the period was that of the jury. The introduction of this "Old Norse" legal institution had been suggested repeatedly from 1814 onward but had been consistently blocked by the government as a "widening of the democratic element of the constitution." Parliament could not, however, be prevented from sending Ole Munch Ræder on his study tour. After the publication of Ræder's report, O. G. Ueland presented an elaborate proposal. In his general justification of the jury system, he partly built on Edward Livingston in emphasizing the sense of "dignity and self-respect" which that kind of responsibility was bound to create in the average citizen. In the long debate which followed, America played a part, particularly in the speeches of Johan Sverdrup, who made the educational value of jury service one of his main arguments. Once more, however, the government refused its sanction.

The third field of impact was education. Interest in the American school system was keen in the Norwegian newspapers all through the nineteenth century, often expressed by eulogies of its democratic character. The main intermediary was Hartvig Nissen (1815-1874), the leading Norwegian school reformer of the period. His American interests were awakened when, in 1851, Parliament sent him to study in Scotland and the United States. However, he never

crossed the Atlantic: he read the Swedish educationist P. A. Silje-
ström's great recent work on the subject and probably found that
he would have little to add. But Nissen studied the book carefully
and wrote an extensive review. He became interested in Horace
Mann and later also became personally acquainted with Mann's
close collaborator, Henry Barnard.

The ideas of these educationists fitted into Nissen's own thought.
He was disturbed by the social mass movements of 1848 and became
convinced that a balanced popular development could be assured
only by the establishment of an elementary school for all children
which would give them what they really needed and educate them
for the fellowship of a living democracy. Nissen had reached such
conclusions on his own, but he was greatly encouraged to find them
expressed so clearly by his American colleagues. No less was he
inspired by the broad popular support which the school enjoyed in
the United States, a support based on local self-government and a
strong associative spirit.

A Danish poet and prophet, N. F. S. Grundtvig, had similar
ideas. He envisaged a "people's high school" which would be closer
to the "folk" and its homely heritage than the Latin-inspired educational institutions of the past. In these visions Grundtvig, too,
found support in America, that "heavenly model of civic liberty."
His influence in Norway was going to be considerable, beginning in
earnest in the 1860s.

The result of these crosscurrents was the law which in 1860 completely transformed the Norwegian elementary school. It was largely
the work of Hartvig Nissen, of whom it has been said that "hardly
any one of the great European school reformers of the time came
so close to Horace Mann's basic ideas."

There were also particular correspondences with American models.
The new schools were to be supported financially both by the government and by the local districts; there was to be no tuition fee.
Parliament passed the latter point following a specific reference to
American conditions. Nissen wanted to break the clerical grip on
education and therefore introduced the system of six (by now, seven-
teen) government-appointed "school directors" for administrative
supervision in each of the great geographic regions; this arrangement Nissen borrowed from the school system in the state of New

York. Following American practice again, he opened Norwegian schools to "modern" subjects such as history, geography, and science, knowledge useful to the grown-up citizen in the present world.

§

CHAPTER 6

Modern America 1861-1914

$\mathbf{T}$he Civil War marks the deepest change in American history. Even before the conflict, Walt Whitman had envisaged a new American continent, physically and morally. During the decades leading up to World War I, this modern America made its appearance.

Its main feature was an expansion with few parallels in history. As American territory reached its present extension, its vastness was filled by mass immigration at an unbelievable speed, and the population was tripled. A similar expansion of industry changed the character of American society. In the course of forty years, production was multiplied by six, and the United States topped the list of the industrial nations.

By itself, this growth gave the country a new economic and political position in the world. At the same time that the physical distance to Europe was reduced by steamships and telegraph, many differences between the two worlds were diminishing no less. Increasingly, both were marked by industrialization, urbanization, middle-class democracy, and rising social unrest, which were the bases for both a new identification and a revival in new forms of old contrasts.

The Civil War divided Europe. Most of the conservatives sympathized with the Confederates. But the delight of more liberal Europeans at the victory of the North proved to be of short duration. Politically, Europe found that it had little to learn from Ulysses Grant's America, and even less from its social Darwinism, corruption, and ruthless economic exploitation, which were climaxed by the bloody clashes of the 1880s. Disappointment was equally strong among European liberals and Marxists. America's aggressive foreign policy in the 1890s and the beginnings of its financial imperialism caused similar misgivings.

These doubts ran parallel to a deeper anxiety. The new America was swiftly developing a new type of commercialized mass civilization, an "American style," which reflected a technical-industrial consumers' society with its conformity, vulgarity, and spiritual confusion. This civilization was just in its beginnings, but through new mass media, it spread with infectious speed, even outside of America, to countries involved in the same transformation. By 1900 Hamburg and Berlin could be called the "most Americanized" among the great cities of Europe. The impact appeared doubly frightening to the European generations of the 1890s, who were turning with disgust from the mechanized modern world toward more spiritual values and saw in the new America a terrifying symbol of their own decay.

Yet much of "old" America survived, and even acquired new relevance under the changed conditions.

During the Civil War, Abraham Lincoln came to represent the best traditions of his nation. In several European democracies, the outcome of the war was felt as an encouragement. The increasing flow of immigrants to the United States—sometimes as much as one million per year—demonstrated the persistence of the American dream among the great masses.

Within the bourgeois class, the fantastic expansion of American economic life confirmed the optimistic ideas of liberalism and was felt as a national inspiration, no less in defeated France and Spain than in imperial Germany. Thomas Edison and Henry Ford became heroes to the world, like Washington and Franklin before. In 1902 William T. Stead proclaimed Americanization to be the desirable aim of all nations.

Even political traditions survived. Liberal Europeans followed with suspense the reform movements in America from the ascendency of Grover Cleveland to that of Woodrow Wilson, and they carefully observed the development of a new and radical social thinking. Philanthropic impulses crossed the Atlantic as before. New American scholarship began making its impact felt; so did American education. Toward the end of the century and after, there were the successive European discoveries of Emerson, Poe, and Whitman and of a new American fiction of social criticism with a worldwide appeal.

European awareness was shown in the beginnings of systematic American studies in the universities. Chairs and institutes were still few and far between, but they demonstrated that America now had to be taken seriously in Europe's own interest. The approach to American studies was now more soberly realistic: the United States was no longer a faraway fata morgana but an expression and a road sign of a civilization increasingly common to the entire Western world.

Norway Follows Suit

Typical of Norway in the same period was an expansion which, on a more modest scale, resembled that of the United States and also created new possibilities of contact across the ocean. Between 1860 and 1914 Norway underwent a transformation unparalleled in its history. Stagnation and poverty were no longer the dominant features. Isolation and self-support yielded to division of labor. The development of a money economy and commerce was supported by fresh capital, including large foreign loans. Modern techniques gained ground incessantly in manufacture and, through a series of booms, made the country a part of the international capitalist economy. In the course of the thirty-five years following 1870, the national product of Norway was almost doubled, and in the following decade it grew at a faster rate than that of the great powers of Europe.

Shipping came first. During a period of less than thirty years, the tonnage was multiplied by five and made Norway third among the sailing nations. Gradually, ships switched from sail to steam, and from 1900 onward, four-fifths of all Norwegian ships ran between foreign ports. Norwegian industry kept time and, toward the end of the century, held a leading position among the Nordic countries, utilizing the numerous waterfalls first by turbines, then by electricity generated by some of the biggest power stations in Europe. Between the years 1850 and 1916, the labor force of Norwegian industry multiplied fourteen times. The same development gradually became typical also of the crafts, agriculture, and fisheries.

The changes made themselves felt in all walks of life, creating a higher living standard, an increase of social mobility, and a new sense of power, in relation to both Sweden and other nations in general. "The nation which once discovered America, now was showing its might on the seven seas." A new national scholarship, painting, and music strengthened the sense of identity. A group of great writers carried the nation's name to the world and played a surprising part in its life at home.

Until the 1880s, much of these released powers were focused on internal politics. In the 1860s the scattered forces of opposition gathered, and the farmers joined the radicals of the urban middle class in the battle for a thorough democratization. Under the leadership of Johan Sverdrup, they forced through one popular reform after another, efficiently limited the power of the bureaucracy, finally made the cabinet responsible to Parliament, and overrode the royal veto by the famous impeachment action of 1884. In 1905, when the Swedes refused to accept the new equality, Norway peacefully canceled the union.

From the 1880s, however, the new economic forces also proved to have further effects which influenced national life no less deeply.

Even though economic growth was rapid, it was not in step with the increase of population. The result was an immense migration, in the first instance internally, from countryside to city. Between the years 1855 and 1910, the population of the capital, Christiania, was multiplied eight times, and the growth rate was similar in other densely populated regions. This migration broke old patterns of life. In the lower classes, it created a sense of displacement and in-

security, and often led to deprivation, economic need, and an unparalleled social tension.

Among the results were changed political constellations: a new
Rightist party, less based on officialdom than on business, a new
Liberal party, bent on social reform, and a Socialist party which
emerged with the sharpening of social contrasts. Democratic optimism, rooted in the Enlightenment, had been a motive force in the
political struggle, but now lost much of its power. Instead, in the
1890s the general European movement of "neoromanticism" made
itself felt, even in Norway, as a reaction against technical efficiency
and rationalism and as a new emphasis on spiritual and national
values.

In this development, even America was now to play a part much
larger than before.

The American Civil War, 1861-1865

The war between the American North and South did not change
America's relationship with Norway, but it made contrasts clearer.

Powerful circles in Europe still hated the American republic and
the ideas behind it. To several of the great powers, the United States
also began to appear as a dangerous rival. The war created economic
difficulties for many nations, above all for the English cotton industry. In Norway, this industry was still weak. On the other hand,
the war strongly stimulated Norwegian shipping, which often replaced, and sometimes even was able to buy, American tonnage.

The joint Norwegian-Swedish minister of foreign affairs openly
expressed sympathy toward the Union cause and forbade the activity
of Confederate purchase agents in the two countries. Formally,
however, the government kept strictly neutral. A Norwegian corvette
protected Norwegian interests in American waters without incident.
But this neutrality did not reflect Norwegian opinion. Intellectual
circles probably were more thrilled by the Polish rebellion in 1863
and the Dano-Prussian War in the following year, but the conflict
in America had a special appeal to the broad layers of the Norwegian
population: relatives and friends were at war there. The interest was
reflected in reprints of *Uncle Tom,* in a melodramatic slavery play,

in a surprising number of historical analyses (some published long after the war), and in the newspapers.

In many ways, the war was bound to appear shocking to Norwegian readers because of the violence of the contrasts, the immense amount of bloodshed, and the sloppiness and corruption on the Union side, which also was referred to in letters from Norwegian volunteers. In the newspapers, there was an increased sense of the strangeness of American conditions and a ruthless will to objectivity, regardless of political coloring.

Indignation about slavery had existed for a long time in Norway, but the division of sympathies in the war was more complicated. There was a certain respect for the Southern love of independence and courage against odds. But, above all, the negative prewar image of political America now came into the picture. There was a widespread suspicion that the Northern love of the Negro covered less lofty interests. During the war, the Norwegian papers repeatedly returned to the well-known rottenness of American (that is, Northern) public life. Even those who strongly sided with the Unionists sometimes wrote about political enthusiasm for America as a matter of the past: "We were deceived by Washington's nimbus." Bull Run might be a foreboding of the end "of the Union, probably also of the Republic."

Morgenbladet, now strongly conservative, took both its war news and its opinions from the English *Times.* But the editor made the real issue clear even before the outbreak of hostilities: the conflict was going to put to the test whether a democratic republic could long exist and whether its principles, moral, intellectual, and economic, were really acceptable. The paper held slim hopes for an "ultrademocratic" nation where the passions of the masses had long ago created a reign of terror, "as foreseen by Tocqueville."

Such ideas were expressed in most drastic form in the journal edited by A. O. Vinje. During the war, he had published in English a highly personal book about British society, and he then planned to go to the United States. His plans did not materialize. But he summed up the sad outcome of the war in terms of history: "Look to this so-called 'land of liberty'!" The republics of classical antiquity had capsized; so would the United States, that caricature of England. Hope for the American republic lacked foundation: "Apparently, the raw beef still needs pounding."

If such a sweeping condemnation is read in its contemporary context, however, it does not represent the main trend of opinion. This holds true even on the Conservative side; *Morgenbladet* itself may serve as an indicator. With all its political bias, its reporting of events in America was often factual and well informed, with a good deal of debate, for which the leaders of both parties were given fair space. Negative judgments often were significantly qualified. But more important, all through the war there was expression of a clearly positive attitude, which probably represented the majority of the population. Largely, it was the libertarian enthusiasm of 1814 which now reasserted itself against the well-known hatred of the conservatives.

Such positive sentiments now acquired additional strength from emigration. It soon became known that Norwegian newcomers to the United States supported the Union cause almost without exception and that well beyond 10 percent of them had entered the Union army as volunteers. As early as 1861, Colonel H. C. Heg organized the famous Scandinavian 15th Regiment from Wisconsin, largely recruited from among Norwegians and with companies called "Othin's Riflecorps" and "The Guard of Henrik Wergeland." Later, the 36th Illinois was also strongly Norwegian. Many of these men made the supreme sacrifice: in the 15th Regiment, casualties ran to almost one-third. There were many war letters to Norway from Union soldiers, and much similar material in the newspapers. It all brought home to the Norwegians what their American compatriots were fighting for.

At the same time, the slavery question also came to arouse a bitter disagreement among the Norwegian immigrants, which at one point even involved the homeland.

The clergy of the immigrant church were largely educated at the highly conservative theological school in Christiania. The church which they organized in America cooperated closely with the equally conservative German synod in Missouri, which was a slave state. Almost all Norwegian immigrants were Republicans; when the war came, many of them began to suspect the attitude of their pastors toward slavery. This suspicion was largely unfounded, but the clergy nourished it by the theological claim that in itself ("as a concept") slavery was not explicitly forbidden in the Holy Scriptures. They added fuel to the fire by advancing conservative arguments commonly used by the Confederates, to the point of condemning as unchristian the idea of natural human rights and even the American Revolution of 1776. Agitation in the congregations was considerable, but the clergy remained adamant. The only pastor to dissent was a chaplain of the 15th Wisconsin Regiment.

In their hour of need, the clergy appealed to their old faculty home in Christiania. The reply, a masterpiece of theological diplomacy, on one side condemned slavery as incompatible with the spirit of Christianity, and on the other condemned as unchristian and sinful "any arbitrary, violent, revolutionary nullification of an historically grown and really existing institution." It is understandable that the Norwegians in America, on both sides of the controversy, received this reply with indignation. It was kept secret until the war was over, when it caused a new battle which lasted until the end of the century.

To our eyes, this conflict must appear as a curious sophistry, but it demonstrates typical traits of the Norwegian immigrant milieu (the Swedes in America experienced nothing of the kind), and also of the religious conservatism at home, which, twenty years later, was going to be mobilized in a similar way in the fight against political "Americanization."

In the case of most Norwegians, however, and in the long run, the great conflict probably was unable to destroy the traditional goodwill toward the United States. Positive sentiments were also supported quite efficiently during the war by American official information, which was distributed through consular channels. There is reason to believe that largely the war was seen as being fought in order to free the blacks, an idea which found its confirmation in the Emancipation Declaration. This view fitted into the image of "good America," whatever the Conservatives might say. Time and again, the sentiment was expressed in declarations of confidence in American democracy, which surely was going to survive. Much more than before, new and disturbing facts now had to be worked into the picture. But the general impression of "health and power" prevailed, and there was a feeling of genuine fellowship with the North, which was perceived as basically different from the South

In Norway, as everywhere in Europe, the person of President Abraham Lincoln aroused little interest to begin with. His murder, however, turned opinion completely even in Norway, and his "immortal glory" also reflected upon his "great and sacred cause." The peaceful transition to another administration was felt to be "a gratifying and useful lesson": the worst misgivings had proved to be without foundation. One of the newspapers probably expressed a general opinion in writing that "the friends of human liberty justly may congratulate themselves on the political results."

In some nations, particularly Great Britain, the outcome of the American Civil War stimulated a policy of democratic reform. In Norway, traditional goodwill, strengthened by emigration, probably was much more important. But from a Norwegian poet of future renown the war called forth a reaction with wide implications.

Henrik Ibsen (1828-1906) early knew the positive liberal image of America, partly from contacts with the circle around Harro Harring and Marcus Thrane. But, like so many others, he changed his opinion during the following years and during the Civil War. In his poem, "The Assassination of Abraham Lincoln," America is described as the home of that anarchical lawlessness which was becoming only too well known to the world.

But to Ibsen, this lawlessness was not distinctive of America. It was an inheritance from old imperialistic Europe, hypocritical and mendacious, steeped in blood and violence. America was just one instance of the general depravation. In its very wildness and primitivism, the country held promise of "the hour of dawn and rejuvenation," when the old system would be "turned inside out" before the great day of judgment.

Few readers noticed this poem at its appearance, but the view of America as primarily an exponent of general forces soon was going to be more widely accepted.

The Great Exodus, 1865-1914

In its dominant features, the contact between Norway and the United States remains identical all through the period 1865-1914, with only a shift of emphasis from the 1890s onward. In particular, this holds true for emigration. The Civil War temporarily checked the movement. People were also deterred by the Indian uprising in Minnesota in 1862 and the massacre at Norway Lake. In 1863 only

1,100 Norwegians left the country for the United States. But in 1866 the figure rose again to almost 15,500, a record so far, and this was only the beginning.

The wave that followed had three crests. The first coincided with the American postwar boom. Between the years 1866 and 1873 about 111,000 Norwegians emigrated, 18,000 in the single year 1869. The next wave ran from 1879 to 1893 and was the largest of all, with a total Norwegian emigration figure of more than a quarter of a million, climaxed in 1882 with 28,800. The final wave, almost equally large, filled the years from 1901 to 1915, when depression in Norway coincided with another American boom; the total figure was 235,000, the apex being the year 1903 with almost 27,000. But also a good many other years after the 1880s showed a figure over 20,000.

Taken altogether, between the years 1866 and 1915, 657,000 Norwegians left for the United States, that is, more than 60 percent of the population surplus. Proportionally, in the decades before 1900, only Ireland shows a higher percentage. Denmark and Sweden are far below.

This immense migration was possible because obstacles were no longer put in its way. Authorities in Norway by now had become completely resigned; in the words of A. M. Schweigaard, "one must submit to the will of Providence." Population increased rapidly also because of a steady drop in the mortality rate. New occupations could absorb only a fraction of the youngsters. There are shocking descriptions from the 1860s, 1870s, and 1880s of need and beggary in the Norwegian countryside. Thus, the American dream appeared as attractive as ever. In 1862 it came true in an unexpected way when the American Congress passed the Homestead Act. To a small farmer from Norway the 160 acres of free soil thus placed at the disposal of each immigrant must have appeared unbelievable. But letters by the hundred thousands confirmed the miracle.

From the 1860s onward, emigration agents added fresh colors to the picture. The consuls of the United States, emissaries from the American and Canadian states, and agents of railroad, shipping, and real estate companies began their propaganda activities in great numbers. In 1882 four steamship lines had a total of more than

1,500 agents at work in Norway. In addition, Norwegian books and pamphlets about emigration prospects appeared in great quantities. All newspapers carried attractive advertisements, and gaudy posters were to be seen in stores.

By all these means of influence, emigration more and more began moving by its own gravity, adhering to its own traditions, and utilizing its own channels of communication. In the 1880s often the tickets of more than half of those who left had been paid for by family or friends in the United States. The "America legend" became infectious, a vision of true adventure and a free and attractive future open to everybody. At springtime, groups of emigrants became an everyday sight in their national costumes and with their rose-painted chests. The sailing of the "America boat" was a popular spectacle, dramatic and moving.

From the 1890s, the movement to some extent changed its character, however. The standard of living was rising fast in Norway. People no longer were escaping from destitution; rather, they were looking for easier circumstances and more promising prospects. The decision to emigrate was not so daring or demanding anymore; most of those who left were assured of a decent income. Emigration became almost normal, like the ordinary work seasons, and no longer sensational. To the younger generation, the United States with its Norwegian settlements was an obvious possibility, and the prospect of working there was often no less attractive than holding a job in a city in Norway; in America, one could work in agriculture as before. In addition, many more now left with the idea of returning to Norway. In the period following 1880, about one-fourth of them did.

Gradually, the movement also changed composition. In the first part of the century, the bulk of the emigrants left by families. Later, the majority increasingly were young and unmarried men. More and more came from the cities and from the new middle class. The phenomenon became less a movement of colonization than a shift within the international labor force, increasingly as mechanical and impersonal as life generally. But its main feature remained. Emigration was the largest upheaval in the history of the Norwegian population and one of its greatest joint experiences.

The "Larger Norway"

The most immediate result of the emigration wave was the development of a "larger Norway" in the United States.

From the beginning, the Norwegians in America mainly settled in six midwestern states. By the year 1900 their number there amounted to almost 700,000, children included. Immediately, in this group, that long process of adaptation began which Th. C. Blegen has named "the American transition." It has been brilliantly described, by him and by Einar Haugen, as a part of American history, to which it rightly belongs.

But in the period under discussion, the survival of a Norwegian heritage still was a dominant feature. The maintenance of national traditions was facilitated by the relative concentration of the settlement. Even more important were the continuous stream of newcomers from the homeland and the impact of the movement for cultural independence in Norway itself. As a result, until World War I a "Norwegian" society existed as a reality in the United States. It was an enclave with vague border lines, and it was involved in continuous change. But to a considerable extent, it followed Norwegian patterns and tried to keep up its ties with Norway.

Instrumental in this struggle were numerous and often impressive cultural institutions: not only the church, but a highly developed school system, many newspapers, several periodicals, and quite a literature, all in Norwegian. Behind these manifestations of identity was a jungle of organizations of all kinds. In retrospect, the effort is pathetic. "Norwegian America" was doomed to become an episode. When immigration dwindled, the group rapidly was absorbed into the English-speaking population. But during these fifty years, its strength was awe-inspiring, the most remarkable instance of Norwegian national self-assertion outside the borders of Norway.

What is largely of interest here, however, is the influence of this Norwegian settlement on that part of the population which did *not* emigrate.

"Official" Norway at the time did not give much thought to the matter. The narrow upper class of the country was often haughty toward the less privileged groups at home, let alone those poor creatures who left for America. Some sporadic sentimentality apart, the Norwegians in the United States and their civilization were regarded with offensive condescension as a transitory phenomenon of minor interest or quite simply ignored.

In the broad layers of population, the situation was different. Family ties, with their continuous flow of everyday information, created a matter-of-course connection with American life unparalleled in the relationship to any other nation. "In my childhood valley in the 1880's," a Norwegian university man recalls,

> I learnt to know the name America before hearing about any other foreign country. And I heard about New York and Chicago before hearing about London and Berlin. Names like Dakota and Minnesota I heard more often than I heard about Spain and France. There were letters all the time, and Norwegian-American newspapers. We read about life on the prairies and in the woods. Every Christmas Norwegian-Americans came home, and told. There were American pictures and books, and American tools. High up in our mountain valley we kept up a lively cultural connection with America. Reports across the ocean widened our intellectual horizon and offered nourishment to our imagination.

Even on a higher level, there were occasional efforts, on both sides of the ocean, to keep cultural contacts, in particular with reference to a common past. From the 1870s, Professor Rasmus B. Anderson (1846-1936) indefatigably reminded his fellow Americans of the Old Norse discovery of America. In 1887-1888, with the support of New England and Norwegian worthies, he succeeded in having statues of Leiv Eiriksson erected in both Boston and Milwaukee. Norwegian-Americans also collected money for national monuments in Norway. In return, in 1893 a Norwegian safely navigated a replica of a Viking ship across the Atlantic to the Chicago exhibition and was warmly received.

Much more important was the influence of "Norwegian America" on everyday life in Norway. The situation was unique: during this half-century, Norway had a transatlantic "colony" with inhabitants who numbered almost one-third of the home population, spoke the Norwegian language, and had a keen interest in maintaining their Norwegian character.

In the end, political interplay did not mean much, nor did direct economic contact. Even culturally, the immigrant group had both limited resources and more pressing tasks. Many of its best forces were lost to the larger American surroundings, and the "Norwegian" milieu itself soon became conservative and retrospective. It developed a sense of alienation from Norway and ceased to serve as a bridge. Nevertheless, to a small nation like Norway, the widening of its cultural territory was bound to be of importance.

Most permanent was the contact between the churches. There was no coordination across the ocean, but a lively mutual interest and a good deal of practical cooperation, particularly in missionary work. Some of the more general influences from American religious life also may have been transmitted to Norway through the emigrants.

In the field of education, the Norwegian group offered few opportunities as yet. When, in the 1850s and 1860s, a modest teaching of Scandinavian languages began in some universities, the staffs were all American. But when it came to books, both church and school in the States long were dependent on supplies from Norway; as late as the 1870s importation was considerable. When production of more current material was taken over by American publishers, great Norwegian writers found a public in the United States. So did new Norwegian periodicals. Norwegian books were reprinted or sold in both countries. Even after 1900, the conductors on the trains in Dakota might offer for sale Norwegian books of the more popular kind. On a higher level, there were early intermediaries, among them R. B. Anderson and, particularly, H. H. Boyesen who emigrated in 1869 and taught at Cornell and Columbia.

The Norwegian milieu also gave elbow room to more special talents. Its cultural organizations were active in the field of theater; Henrik Ibsen's *Ghosts* was given its world premiere by a Norwegian amateur group in Chicago. Quite a number of actors who later were to gain fame at home in Norway began their careers on such simple stages. A number of virtuosi of the Norwegian national fiddle, and also some musicians of the more traditional kind, toured the settlements in the Middle West. A few pictorial artists studied and worked in the Norwegian milieu, which also offered support to champions in typical Norwegian sports, such as skating and skiing. Most Norwegian writers who visited America naturally found their first contacts in Norwegian-speaking settlements.

The Wider Impact—Economics, 1865-1914

The Norwegian group in the United States was, however, a minor segment within a much larger picture.

As before, official contacts between the two countries remained unimportant. The number of Norwegians among the Norwegian-Swedish ambassadors to Washington slowly grew, and their number on the consular level also increased, but there was no special Norwegian foreign policy. When ex-President Ulysses Grant visited Norway in 1878, the Norwegian-Swedish king happened to be in Christiania and lionized the honored guest. But such occasions were rare. The real impact was economic and was partly connected with emigration.

The negative side weighs heavily here. In this period, the population of Norway grew more slowly than was the case generally in Western and Northern Europe, and in the heaviest emigration years it decreased. In some districts, emigration much exceeded the surplus of births for years in succession. Until World War I, Norway had fewer young men and more women, children, and elderly persons than most nations. Among those who left were many individuals marked by initiative and young daring—an incalculable loss.

Even more important was the negative impact on the very life of the people. Emigration from Norway formed part of a general breaking up of social patterns which was accompanied by a restless sense of uncertainty, a lack of commonly accepted standards, and a spiritual confusion that may well be compared to that of contemporary America. The large-scale movement of population hit poor and sparsely populated areas with particular violence and often left them hopeless and semi-paralyzed. Emigration to America was not the only, or even the largest, element in that process, but it was the most dramatically visible part and often was a direct continuation of it; among the emigrants from the cities, probably more than half had first moved from the countryside. By its character of unorganized exodus, the flight across the ocean emphasized the general sense of atomization, each individual on his own, at the mercy of capricious forces.

But there was also a certain compensation. The departure of 10,000 to 15,000 youngsters every year made labor more valuable at home. Wages rose steadily, employers had to pay some attention to demands from their workers, and social pressure subsided. The change increased social unrest, intensified the contrast between the generations, and strengthened a general radicalism and urge for independence both politically and otherwise.

Even more clearly positive were the direct economic consequences.

In 1913 a government committee maintained that, generally speaking, the population movement across the sea had not involved any loss to Norway in dollars and cents because of the money sent home by the emigrants. This statement can hardly be proved, but, doubtless, this "return money" ran to considerable amounts. As an example, in the year 1901 the American money sent home to one of the Norwegian counties with strong emigration exceeded the tax assessment of that year in all the municipalities taken together. In 1905 the total amount returned to Norway was around 20 million Norwegian crowns and equaled the value of the entire Norwegian import from the United States that year. (The entire Norwegian government budget in 1905 ran to less than 100 million.) In addition, there was the money inherited or willed for public endowments every year, again by the millions. In 1920 there were almost 50,000 Norwegians who had returned from the United States for permanent residence in the homeland. In addition to their working power, most of them also brought back considerable savings.

In the tremendous expansion of Norwegian shipping after the American Civil War, freight to and from the United States was the dominant feature. In the course of eighteen years, transatlantic trade was multiplied at least twenty times. For a few years, emigration played a considerable part in that expansion. Beginning in the 1870s, Norwegian sailing vessels were knocked out of the competition for passenger traffic by foreign steamers. However, Norwegian bulk carriers became dominant in the transport of goods for which speed was less essential: lumber; coal; from the 1860s, petroleum; and, somewhat later, grain. In the year 1879, 1,128 Norwegian ships arrived in New York; often there were from fifty to one hundred Norwegian vessels or more in the harbor at one time. Even here, for a while Norway could not compete with foreign steamships, but after 1900, the fleet was modernized. In 1913 American ports were visited by about 2,300 Norwegian ships.

In industry, American inventions played a prominent part. Norway built its National College of Technology only in 1910. Until then, Norwegian engineers were educated in Sweden, Germany, and Switzerland; Norwegian technical journals of the time largely refer to German and British sources, but from the 1880s, there was a change. Important were the great American exhibitions, beginning with the one in Philadelphia in 1876, at which Norway was officially represented by a warship and a special pavillion. A number of Norwegian representatives to the exhibition published reports, particularly about the technical wonders, and found that in these fields America was now "surpassing Europe with astonishing superiority."

A sign of this new orientation was the emigration to the United States of Norwegian engineers, many of them graduates from the best European colleges. More than seven hundred left the country for America, representing the highest qualified group among Norwegian emigrants. A good many of them came to hold leading positions in American technology. But their departure was not a complete loss. Quite a few returned or shuttled between Norway and America. They became essential intermediaries between the United States and the "fruitful technical milieu" in Norway at the end of the century.

The details of this American impact have not been investigated and in themselves are hard to ascertain. In this period, many inventions were "in the air," were developed almost simultaneously in several countries, or were further developed in Europe before reaching Norway. The impact itself is obvious, however, and can be indicated by the number of leading Norwegian industrialists who for some period worked in the United States. Often they belonged to a new group of experts outside the old circle of mill owners.

Among individual fields in which America was influential may be mentioned metallurgy, mining, shipbuilding, the oil industry, the production of canned goods, the construction of harbors, roads, bridges, and railways, and general contracting. And these are just examples. Even American military technique was influential, such as John Ericsson's ironclad *Monitor.* The Cuban war in 1898 was followed by a Norwegian study commission. One of the members, later a Norwegian minister of defense, used his experience at Santiago for the construction of the line of fortifications along the Swedish border which played a part in the dissolution of the union with Sweden in 1905.

Central to the development of industry was the problem of power, however, since Norway had no coalfields. Instead, water power was used, mainly for the production of lumber, wood pulp, and paper. The invention of the turbine engine created a revolution. Leading Norwegian experts in the field went to the United States for training and returned with the idea of creating "Niagaras in Norway."

Even more decisive were developments in the use of electricity. The first Norwegian telegraph line (1855) probably followed European adaptations of Samuel Morse's ideas. But the first telephone was sent home to Norway from the Philadelphia exhibition one year after Alexander Graham Bell's invention of it and was put to use soon thereafter. Electric light was early produced by arc lamps, and a power station for Edison's incandescent lamp was built right away in Hammerfest, the northernmost city of the world. Plans for an electric tramway were formulated in Christiania the year after its invention in America, and in the early 1890s the government studied the electrical railroads in the United States.

But it was the hydroelectric industry which was going to influence Norwegian life most deeply. The pioneer plant, the electrochemical Norsk Hydro, was based on a Norwegian invention, but previous American experiments had offered one of the starting points. Some of the leading men in this field had long experience from American industry and later became professors at the National College of Technology.

There was a similar impact within the traditional Norwegian fields of occupation. New American tools and machines, from the sewing machine to the linotype, affected old handicrafts. Sometimes they facilitated the transition to industrial production, sometimes they created mass unemployment which was relieved only by emigration. There was a keen interest in American fishing methods, such as hatching, but above all in the construction of tools for use in the deep sea. After abortive imitations, practical models of a fishing steamer with purse net and small dories were brought to Norway from Philadelphia in 1876. The results proved excellent, and soon the technique was applied everywhere by Norwegian fishermen. The same held true of the first open motorboat.

In agriculture, the United States proved to become an important factor indirectly. While Norway lived mostly on foreign grain, it imported only small quantities from America. But because of the immense harvests in the United States and the low freight rates, grain prices went down all over the world. The ordinary Norwegian consumer did not mind, but for Norwegian farmers grain production now became unprofitable. They switched to cattle breeding and feed and dairy production, which called for the use of machines. The increased wages caused by the population movement also had effect. With fewer hands needed, emigration soared even more, swiftly reducing the number of cotters and making the farms rely more and more on the working power of the family.

America also played a part in agricultural mechanization. Particularly after the Philadelphia exhibition in 1876, American tools made their triumphant entry into Norway; for example, between the years 1875 and 1907, the number of mowing machines and reapers multiplied almost forty times. Many of the machines were American-made. Also, American methods of cultivation were tried and sometimes adopted successfully. Returning Norwegian-Americans often proved to represent a practical initiative in their home districts. Having gained useful experience in the United States, both women and men were eager to apply their knowledge and use their new tools in the more traditional milieu of their origin.

The impact of these factors should not be exaggerated, however. It was tramp shipping that influenced Norwegian economic life most decisively. Direct exchange of goods across the ocean certainly increased in the period, but still was far below the figures for Germany and Great Britain, for example. Even less impressive was the importation of American capital. A few American firms established branch offices in Norway, but there was no investment in new enterprises. The huge hydroelectric development in the new century was largely financed by foreign capital, but hardly any came from American sources. Both money and machinery still were European.

To the common man, it was bound to mean much more that during these decades American everyday articles for the first time began entering the Norwegian market. As was the case with technical innovations, exact analysis is difficult. Many of these goods reached the country in European variants. Very soon some of them also came into production in Norway itself, and nobody remembered their origin. But quite a number doubtless made their appearance before World War I.

Some goods introduced to Norway have already been noted, including kerosene, which of course was used for both light and cooking. Others include the elevator. Most were practical inventions for home or office. The range was immense, from safety pin, fountain pen, and safety razor to gas stove, vacuum cleaner, and refrigerator. Before long it became incomprehensible how business could ever have been carried on without the use of typewriter and duplicator, cash register and calculating machine. In addition came phonograph and camera, and soon after 1900, most important of all, the movie projector.

Other American articles appeared as well, now in quantity, from victuals and wines to textiles, furniture, and nostrums. Even the American entertainment industry put out its first feelers.

The Wider Impact—Culture, 1865-1914

The increasing inflow of everyday American products gradually made the country lose its touch of the strange and miraculous. It took its natural place among the other great powers.

This shift is noticeable in the field of scholarship. As universities in the United States became better organized, contacts were established where needs arose. American humanities still remained practically unknown until the turn of the century. But there was a growing interest in the social sciences, and after the Civil War, American medicine was taken seriously. The leading Norwegian surgeon of the time, Professor Julius Nicolaysen (1831-1909), spent the year 1867-1868 in the United States and ever after showed the marks of his experience. He was followed by many other Norwegian physicians within various branches of medicine, in particular in odontology. A number of Norwegians, including several future professors, studied in "the Eldorado of dentistry."

The impact of American science was also felt toward the end of the nineteenth century, both in popularization and in scholarly studies. After 1900, a number of outstanding Norwegians worked in the United States in physics, geology, biology, and meteorology or participated in American voyages of discovery. Before 1900, the Norwegian Academy of Sciences for years had only one American member, the Norwegian-born zoologist L. H. Stejneger, curator of the Smithsonian. But during the following fourteen years, ten other American scientists were elected members.

American pictorial arts still were little known, but at least one Norwegian painter, O. P. H. Balling, made a career in America, not least by numerous portraits of Presidents Lincoln and Grant. More important, many Norwegian artists were represented in the great American exhibitions, from the World Fair in Philadelphia in 1876 to the New York Armory Show in 1913, and thus gained access to an international audience. Outstanding Norwegian musicians worked successfully in the United States both as performing artists and as conductors or were invited as visiting professors to American institutions of music. Henrik Ibsen, at least, was played by all American professional theaters.

Many humanitarian movements of American origin in these years received a fresh, additional impetus from their homeland. Abstinence from alcohol was given a strong religious motivation by the organization in Norway in 1877 of the Independent Order of Good Templars (IOGT); in 1920 a Norwegian was even elected Chief Templar. In the 1880s similar organizations were founded for women. There was much cooperation across the ocean in these matters, and American ideas became important to Norwegian social reform. This holds true for the local option system, introduced in Norway in 1894, according to which liquor licenses are granted or not granted in local referendum. The idea of a general prohibition of alcohol was keenly discussed for decades, using America as an example, until the reform was realized in 1916, only to be dropped again eleven years later, as it was in the United States.

By far the most important cultural influence in the period came from religious movements.

Mormonism still caused some wild polemics. In 1879 the American government asked Norway-Sweden to stop all Mormon emigration to the United States. This demand was rejected, but even without such interference the sect now gradually dwindled into relative insignificance.

A totally different influence emanated from the various Lutheran denominations in the United States. Of special importance was the translation after the Civil War of American religious literature of all kinds. The Norwegian-American churches probably often served as intermediaries. These books were widely read, and most of the great American contemporary writers of spiritual works figure on the list, which was topped in the 1890s by the famous Charles M. Sheldon (twelve books translated). But besides such general influence there was now also an impact from new American sects. Common to all of them were a typical "American style," a "low church" atmosphere, a free and informal sermon, and a strong strain of revivalism.

A forerunner was the "movement of sanctification," which believed in cure by prayer. It was spread over the world by the Swedish-American lay preacher Fredrik Franson, who was also widely read in Norway and left his mark in Björnstjerne Björnson's religious drama *Beyond Human Power* (1883). More practically efficient were the Seventh Day Adventists, members of a millennial church which came to Norway in 1878 and soon became firmly established with publications, schools, clinics, and sanatoriums; it maintained close cooperation with its American headquarters. More loosely organized were the "Russellites," or Witnesses of Jehovah, active in Norway since 1903 and in strength approximately on the same level as the Adventists.

The Baptist and Methodist churches long ago had become firmly rooted in Norway and continued growing until World War I, when recruitment stagnated. Their offspring, the more ecstatic Pentecostal Movement, got under way in 1907 and, during the following half-century, became the largest free church in Norway.

The impact which exerted the strongest general influence also had its roots in Methodism. From the 1870s onward, the lay preacher Dwight Lyman Moody and the hymnist and singer I. D. Sankey worked as a revivalist team all over the United States and Great Britain. Both in sermons and song they represented something revolutionary: nobody before had presented the gospel in such a striking and popular way. Their writings and songs immediately became extremely popular in Norway. By 1920, about fifty books by and about Moody and many collections of Sankey's songs had appeared in Norwegian, often in large printings.

In the twentieth century, this impact gained an unparalleled force. Two young Norwegian lay preachers had worked in the United States in the spirit of Moody and upon their return started "the revival of 1905," one of the strongest mass movements of the time. Simultaneously, another disciple of Moody, John R. Mott, gave new life to the YMCA organization and had a noticeable influence even in Norway. A more pietistic youth movement called Christian Endeavor came to Norway from America about the same time and worked along similar lines.

Within the organized churches of dissenters in Norway, America has thus been a motive force of decisive importance. About three-fourths of the present membership in such churches belong to denominations which have a background in the United States. This hardly amounts to more than 3 percent of the total population of Norway, but the real influence is much stronger and goes beyond the border lines of organization. Some essential traits of American church life proved unsuitable; in Norway, religious membership never became a sign of social status as it did in the United States. But in a more general way, the American impact gradually changed the very character of the Norwegian state church. It created a new tradition of song and a new style in the sermons. Above all, it made revival and personal religious experience more important than the sacraments to a great number of Norwegian Christians.

Fresh Judgments, 1865-1885

But besides such relatively neutral traits, material and cultural, there was also, as before, a continuous stream of American impressions and impulses that were highly controversial and were felt as a challenge to judgment and action in the day-to-day conflicts within Norway itself. The contrasts were brought out clearly during the Civil War and even much more so during the years that followed. The two decades preceding the middle 1880s were marked by disagreements of a violence rarely paralleled in Norwegian history; large parts of the population were raised against one another in bitter struggles. Here America again became an active element.

The interplay was facilitated by a steadily increasing flow of information. The single university of Norway at the time still played a modest part in this development, and in some respects a negative one. American geography now was competently covered in teaching, and the political struggles called for a fresh interest in American constitutional law. From 1873 there also was a professorship in English and Romance philology. The first incumbent, Johan Storm (1836-1920), was a pioneer in his emphasis on the present-day spoken tongue; in that connection, he made important studies of the American idiom. But the practical result of his "direct method" of teaching was an exclusive concentration on British pronunciation, literature, and civilization, which dominated both university and secondary schools until after World War II.

In the newspapers, the only mass medium of the time, however, the situation now improved. Still, the news service was largely indirect and coverage uneven. But the very quantity of American material grew noticeably after the Civil War. At the same time, the increased intensity of the political conflict in Norway made the newspapers even more eager to use the United States as a weapon in internal battles.

"A Picture Somber and Sinister"

The image of America thus presented in day-to-day reporting at first glance appears strongly negative, and for good reasons. Except for the 1920s and 1960s, the "Gilded Age" probably was the least edifying period in American history and was felt as such even in Europe. Norwegian papers wrote extensively about all the seamy sides of American life: the lack of political leadership, the dominance of "machines" and big money, the corruption and wanton destruction of values, the racial discrimination, the ruthless exploitation of labor, the "system of fraudulence" and humbug, and the cultural insipidity and standardization covered up by a destructive restlessness.

This image no longer could be disregarded as hostile propaganda by one political faction, and it was bound to appear particularly disheartening for that reason. Even the newspapers of the opposition now spoke their minds without inhibition about the "fundamental flaws" of the American republic. In 1867 the chief ideologist of the Liberal party, the historian J. E. Sars (1835-1917), wondered whether a new civil war was in the offing in America. In the following year he saw the acquittal of President Andrew Johnson as "a unique spot of light in the somber and sinister picture presented today by America's state of affairs." On the Conservative side, *Morgenbladet* warned against unreliable derogation of American life and sometimes praised the country wholeheartedly. The more convincing were its shocking reports, doubly because the American horrors were often referred to as though they were known to everybody.

Norwegians also began to be apprehensive about the foreign policy of the new great power. During the Civil War, rumors of an American-Russian understanding now were combined with the fact that after the war Tsar Nicholas I expressed a wish for a Russian harbor in the Norwegian North. In 1867 there was a nervous question in the Swedish Parliament about this "sudden friendship." In the following year, a summer tour of the northern provinces by the American minister to Stockholm aroused such suspicions in the papers that the American government found reason to issue an official disavowal of any sinister conspiracy.

In the broadest layers of the population of Norway, another source of information came into the picture at this time: a new type of vulgar literature, the American "cock-and-bull" stories. The genre made a sudden start in the 1870s, saw its culmination after 1890, and, with its last offshoots, reached down into the interwar period. It began with two competing series both entitled *American Tales* (respectively, twenty and fourteen volumes, many of them in several editions), followed by three similar series "from all countries'' but often with American subjects; one of the latter series ran to eighty-six volumes. The 1890s added two series called *American Crime (Detective) Stories,* two similar series under different names, and many individual books of the same kind.

This literature concerned two areas: Indian and frontier life, and the milieu of bandits and gangsters. Some of the authors were American writers of some fame, such as Edward S. Ellis and Max Pemberton. But most of them were anonymous, and quite a number were German. They describe a colorful, sensational, and lawless America. The Indian books moved from the original savages to the Wild West with Buffalo Bill and Jesse James, and also for good measure threw in piracy on the Mississippi and life in the gold fields. Urban scoundrels were described with no less variation. After 1900, literary demands were rising. Gradually, the original genre was degraded to penny-booklets about Sitting Bull, Nick Carter, Nat Pinkerton, and Ethel King, ''queen of the women detectives.''

This literature was international and satisfied the desire for reading in new groups of population. But it also fitted into, confirmed, and exploited the image of an exotic, grotesque, and wild United States. Typically, it was accompanied by a production of original Norwegian tales of the same kind, written on both sides of the ocean, some of them by authors of future renown. They all built on the same notions, by now firmly rooted in the popular mind. When, in the 1860s, a slum district developed in Christiania, ''at an American speed'' and with ''crazy living conditions,'' it was baptized ''New York'' by the man in the street, and not without reason.

This image of America now also could be used conveniently for political purposes. Party lines were clearly drawn, again most typically in *Morgenbladet*, but with a significant dichotomy. On one side, the United States remained the great demonstration of the depravity of that democracy which was the program of the Liberal party. On the other side, the Rightists now also discovered a conservative America, which had often been overlooked, but which surely deserved attention as well in present-day Norway.

The negative features of America most often appeared in the presentation of the news and the comments on it, but also in general statements and direct polemics. Most weighty was a series of twenty extremely well informed articles written between 1871 and 1873 in *Morgenbladet* by an unknown Norwegian living in the United States. In great detail he confronted, point by point, the "unattainable model of perfection" presented by "our Americanized fellow countrymen" and the American realities as he saw them. The articles led up to the conclusion that "when it comes to internal political life, Norway is much to be preferred to the United States."

Events in America in the 1870s and 1880s repeatedly evoked similar reflections. The railway strike in 1877 was compared to the Paris Commune. The murder of President Garfield rubbed in the same truths, corroborated by condemning quotations from a new American writer, Henry George. The newspapers charged that the jury system in Chicago had become a farce in a milieu where "good and honest men are exceptions," and that universal suffrage in the United States had proved disastrous, a fact obvious to "all people of property, education and honor." In 1883 *Morgenbladet* triumphantly reported that the old labor leader Marcus Thrane, on a visit to his homeland, now expressed his deep disappointment with the American republic.

Such statements were not only sweeping in content but were also often presented with a note of insulting snobbery. *Morgenbladet* once wrote that America was the place where a poor tailor might become president and where people could place their feet on the table and scratch themselves the way they liked. "The idea is," a Liberal writer bitingly retorted, "that in America live the scoundrels, in Paris the Communards, Wisdom in Christiania and Virtue in Stockholm." No wonder that through the years many newspapers, both in the United States and Norway, wrote protests, raging against such "American" reports with their political bias.

Even American institutions found worthy of praise on the Conservative side were seen largely as indispensable brakes within a play of lawless forces. But those forces now increasingly were showing their brazen face even in Norway, and the same remedies recommended themselves there.

As it had to Christian Magnus Falsen, the American Senate again appeared in a favorable light, together with a cabinet independent of congressional whim and a presidential veto that had real importance. Equally commendable to Norwegian Conservatives were the attempts in America "to limit the competence of the deliberating bodies, and to concentrate power in the hands of certain higher officials''—the speaker and the committees in Congress, the governors in the states, the mayors in the municipalities, and the judges in court. The Supreme Court and its judicial review crowned the hierarchy of power.

The most balanced discussion of the subject is a pamphlet by a professor of law, Bernhard Getz (1850-1901), perhaps the most brilliant brain on the Conservative side. He knew American constitutional law and the European discussion of it thoroughly, and he was no reactionary. The main flaw in the American system in his view was unrestricted suffrage. But the defects were counterbalanced by the existence of a Senate which expressed the views of the top layer of society, an effective suspensive veto by the president and state governors, and a slow and complicated procedure of constitutional amendment. Taken together, these restrictive powers were able to moderate the dominance of the absolute majority, providing a model for other nations.

"Land of Blessing"

American ideas did not engage the right wing in the political struggle in Norway only in the context of Norway's internal affairs; they were also used in reply to that positive image of America that now once again was hoisted as a banner by the other side.

What reappeared, with the power of a new situation, was the old ideology from the youth of Henrik Wergeland. A good many new and unpleasant facts by now had to be worked into the image, but they were not allowed to become more than shadows in a picture that was drawn mainly in bright colors. It was based on no less factual realities than was its counterimage. The sweeping victories of American ideas leave little doubt what views were backed by the majority of the Norwegian people.

The broad foundation of these sentiments was of course the continually rising tide of emigration. Doubtless, the bulk of letters sent home after the Civil War reported a growing prosperity. They also could tell about a beginning political influence in the new country: in 1875 the Norwegian Knute Nelson started his brilliant career in a local legislature and the U.S. Senate. Norwegian-American news-papers publicized such facts widely; as late as 1950, _Decorah-Posten_ had a circulation in the homeland of 4,000. Among the Norwegian farm population, in the lower classes in town, and also in large parts of the new middle class, a relatively positive image of America probably by now was both well known and fully accepted.

The picture was added to by a growing literature of popular in-formation, not only the translation of a solid German geography of America (1881) and historical popularizations of various kinds, but also a number of Norwegian books and travel accounts about con-temporary America. They varied a good deal, both in their objec-tivity and bias, but largely brought out the image of "a land of blessing."

The individual who at this early date placed such material most clearly within the framework of day-to-day Norwegian politics was the opposition leader Sören Jaabæk. In 1865 he began the publica-tion of a newspaper which served as the mouthpiece of his mighty organization of farmers. It was possibly the Norwegian paper with the widest circulation at the time, and besides an American history ("The Great Republic"), it reported current news from America in practically every issue.

Jaabæk was not blind to the darker sides of American metropol-itan life, but most of his readers were cotters and owners of small Norwegian farms; therefore, he largely described the life of the average settler in the Middle West. Taken together, the articles amounted to an almost complete list of those advantages that now, for almost half a century, had drawn the common man from Norway to the United States. Implicitly, they also summed up in primitive simplicity what shortcomings should correspondingly be remedied at home. Jaabæk justly wrote that "my American reports are a part of my policy." His newspaper was a continuous confrontation of the land of Franklin and Lincoln and present-day Norway: "Helas, we will have to wait for a long time before the ideas of liberty have in a similar way penetrated _our_ life."

The image of America among other groups of the opposition movement had more variety and sophistication but essentially pointed to the same values. Self-government was seen as the essence of American political life; it was exercised in direct election of most officials, wide political information, and open campaigning, which turned the institutions of government into schools of civic education. To Norwegians who held this view, criticism of America largely sprang from hatred and envy. Emigrants, in their letters home, demonstrated that in America, they had gained "a new respect as human beings."

Björnson himself, in an article in 1873 in a Norwegian-American newspaper, declared that, in all the reform movements along Jaabæk's line, emigration had been a motive power and the image of America a continuous force, both pointing toward the ultimate goal: "the complete reign of the parliament."

In the Liberal press, current political events in the United States were interpreted in the same spirit of democratic fellowship. In 1868 the skeptical J. E. Sars saw the election of "honest and firm" Ulysses Grant as president as a guarantee that the results of the Civil War would not be lost. In 1881 a Liberal paper marked the news of President Garfield's death with a black border: he had "a mission of reform." Cleveland was greeted as a presidential candidate: he was a man of the people!

This confidence in the resilience of American democracy was found among liberals all over Europe, and these attitudes were known in Norway also. Édouard Laboulaye, a professor at the Collège de France, was a courageous advocate of American libertarian ideas all through the Second Empire. Part of his *American History* was translated into Norwegian. Extracts from his witty, imaginative novel *Paris en Amérique* (1863), confronting ossified France with young America, were printed in translation in a Norwegian newspaper in 1864; in 1872 the novel appeared in full in another newspaper and in 1877 as a book.

At the same time, however, there was a definite shift of emphasis toward a different part of the gospel of progress; the change was noticeable even before the Civil War, but now steadily gained in strength. Jaabæk represented the small farmers and their relatively limited view; he was rather hostile to the growth of industrial and urban society. Other groups hoped for the same political reforms but were no less fascinated by the immense economic expansion typical of modern America. In 1884 one of the few liberal professors at the University of Christiania wrote that Norwegians should learn from the Americans to "become an industrial nation, like the Swiss, and break with the old so-called idealism."

But equally striking was the bourgeois, middle-class attitude toward these problems. Norwegian industrialism still was in its beginnings, and the country far removed from the ideas of Karl Marx. In this respect, there was still little, if any, difference between Conservatives and Liberals. In 1865 *Morgenbladet* extolled America as the homeland of free competition. On this point, the paper probably was fully endorsed by the opposition.

Both parties occasionally expressed their horror at the "excesses of competition" and the "secret power of Wall Street." But there was only censure of misuse, never a criticism of the system itself— it had made America's progress possible. "Help yourself" was accepted as the American slogan, and without objections. A Liberal paper discussed the many communist experiments in the United States, but just as "aberrations." Another Liberal paper found with relief that the railroad strike in America in 1877 proved to have had "no political or communist character." Rather, the outcome demonstrated "an auspicious solidity of social conditions" due to "the democratic constitution."

An odd part was played in this regard by the old classic, Benjamin Franklin: his economic philosophy now could be regarded as a social panacea. There was a continued interest in his writings and biography with their bourgeois moralism. One translation of *Poor Richard* in 1877 had the title *Time and the Workman*. Another translation in the same year was recommended in J. E. Sars's periodical for distribution to the labor class: if Franklin's lessons in saving were listened to, then "the future would see less of need and squalor in town and countryside."

This social unanimity beneath the day-to-day conflicts was curiously brought out by ex-President Grant's visit to Christiania in 1878, the year after the bloody American railroad strike. Jaabæk had always admired Grant and his simple manner. In his newspaper, he happily reported how Grant was not only received by the king but cheered by "the people" and greeted with "flags from the houses of several republicans."

Grant's statement to the Norwegian press was felicitous, a George Washington resurrected. He praised the Norwegians in the United

States, "good and faithful Republicans almost all of them." He condemned Napoleon III but praised Holland, which was, he said, in reality a republic, but without demagogues and socialists. He stated that, even in America, the "social trouble-makers" were mainly immigrants and were now being repelled by "the classes of property." He made these remarks to *Morgenbladet,* but his words pleased Jaabæk no less.

The fightingly positive attitude toward America on the Liberal side was further strengthened during these decades by cultural movements with an American background. So far, they had appeared as mildly humanitarian and relatively harmless. From the 1860s and 1870s onward, they appeared with a new aggressiveness, as part of a radical modernism with political implications.

The American movement for the emancipation of women had so far been regarded with a somewhat platonic sympathy in Norway, which was at a safe distance. What definitely tied these ideas to the new radicalism and at the same time gave them an intensively personal character was, of course, John Stuart Mill's book on the subject. It was translated into Danish in 1869 by the firebrand Georg Brandes, discussed extensively in Björnson's newspaper in the following year, and called forth political action right away. But the person who made the problem a matter of general public debate was the woman painter Aasta Hansteen (1824-1908).

She was a feminist from her girlhood on and early sought contact with her American fellow fighters. In the 1870s she took up her own public battle for, among other things, marriage legislation of the American type. She did so in a mannish and reckless way which highly provoked the bourgeoisie. Tired of badgering and derision, she left for "the free West" in 1880 and stayed for nine years. She moved in the highest feminist circles; one of her paintings is called "Europe Pays Homage to American Women." She was shaken by social conditions in the metropolitan United States, but she never lost her faith in the country where "even the genteel are broadminded."

At the same time, a new school of great writers in Norway raised the banner of feminism, with continued reference to the United States. In 1884 the Liberal politician H. E. Berner (1839-1920) and the future leader of the feminist movement Gina Krog (1847-1916) together outlined a practical strategy, directly based on the American experience. In its vitriolic counterattacks, the clergy retorted by referring to America as licentious because of its many abortions. They were answered in books and articles from a new generation of feminists: in the emancipation of woman, as in other respects, America was "the stirring omen of social justice." Even the American battle for a reform of women's clothes now had repercussions in Norway.

A Norwegian feminist periodical ran for forty years from 1887 onward, presenting a current report of American feminism and of international cooperation in the field. And not only did the cause find support on the left; among its wholehearted spokesmen was a future Conservative prime minister, who on this point hailed the American "reckless disregard of all social barriers and prejudices."

By the middle 1880s, public debate had paved the way for political decision about the rights of women. The same preparation took place in the field of school reform. Demands became increasingly vocal for a school adapted to the new type of society which was taking shape. America formed an important part of that society.

Some of the impact was indirect, coming through Denmark. After the Civil War, the ideas of Grundtvig more and more made themselves felt in Norway, with America as one of the examples. There the schools were really built on "equality and liberty." They gave everyone the foundation he needed. They did not work by cramming, report cards, and religious education. Teaching was free and close to life, and created in pupils a frankness and intrepidity unknown on the European side of the ocean.

In the 1860s, Grundtvig's "people's high schools" had their breakthrough in Norway, heralded by Christopher Bruun (1839-1920). Bluntly, he pointed to America in contrast to the "black" Latin tradition of decrepit Europe. In the United States Bruun saw a "manly fearlessness," a vigor and common sense, a respect for all kinds of work, and a close contact between the classes. Such qualities also had something to do with the educational system and were going to be an ideal for the many schools of the new type in Norway.

Within the traditional system of education, Hartvig Nissen remained the dominant figure through much of the period. In his appreciation of American education he was now joined by another reformer, Peter Voss (1837-1909), whose journal of pedagogy became an arsenal of progressive educational thought. These ideas were felt as part of the general wave of radicalism and were met by well-known reactions on the Conservative side: the school in the United States was just another side of the general American decadence and "not in any respect" worthy of imitation, least of all in its comprehensive organization and its coeducation. When anarchy and disintegration eventually made their entry in America and "the dikes of the Constitution are washed away," one of the critics wrote, much of the blame would have to be placed on the frivolous school system.

But equally strong were the positive reactions. The German Friedrich Oetken's sympathetic little book on the subject was translated in 1881. The professional journals and many of the newspapers showed a similar attitude, sometimes in aggressive comparison with Norwegian conditions. Björnson's paper contrasted Cornell University in America with the "rusty and moss-covered" institutions in Norway.

At the center of interest was the elementary school, not yet with respect to the pedagogical details as much as the organization. Most important in the context was Hartvig Nissen's book about the schools in Massachusetts, published in 1868 at public expense. What above all inspired Nissen in the American situation was the truly democratic spirit as expressed in local self-government, the strict separation of church and state, and the elevating general generosity toward educational institutions. Through the American material, Nissen pointed to desirable reforms at home, and he himself managed to carry out some of them, such as special economic support for sparsely populated districts. But no less important in a general way was the wide circulation of his book.

With regard to higher education, Nissen strongly favored the American comprehensive system, according to which the secondary school is based on the elementary school and common to all social classes. After Nissen's death, Peter Voss continued his struggle, with frequent references to the United States. The battle also came to turn around the question of whether coeducation should be introduced into the secondary schools. Behind it was, of course, the general problem of woman's place in society. Both Peter Voss and others here made available to the public extensive American material, particularly as put together by John Eaton. Some of these Norwegian reports on the subject were weighty enough to be translated in Germany and the United States. Also, in his strivings for other reforms, Voss clearly drew on pedagogical experience in America.

Behind the disagreements there were often conflicting general views of life. Here the catchwords did not come from the United States; there were sources nearer home. Nevertheless, even American freethinkers played their part. When, in the late 1870s, Björnson broke with Christianity, he followed European masters. But when he later visited the United States, he became acquainted with American critics of the Bible. He had a book by Charles B. Waite translated into Norwegian and he published, with a preface by himself, a collection of articles by the well-known agnostic Robert G. Ingersoll which was reprinted twice and was followed by two more books by Ingersoll. Björnson even toyed with the idea of a transatlantic periodical for such criticism. Again the United States took its place on the radical side.

American creative writing also benefited from these discussions. Norway here was late, as compared, for instance, with Sweden. There was some knowledge and a few translations of the New England classics. But A. O. Vinje felt most of this literature to be third or fourth rate, and Longfellow "stale and affected." Gradually the new realists, Mark Twain and Bret Harte, added fresh colors to the picture. In the 1880s, the first translations of William Dean Howells and Henry James made their appearance, and in 1882 even Henry Adams's political novel *Democracy.*

The Norwegian Writers

Norwegian authors, however, were going to play the most important part when it came to the dissemination of American ideas.

In the great battles of the period their contribution was extraordinary, even in molding the image of the United States. Some of their books were "pure" literature. But the most important writers repeatedly took a stand in the conflicts of the day and used the American material accordingly. Only once the so-called "four masters," Henrik Ibsen, Björnstjerne Björnson, Alexander L. Kielland, and Jonas Lie, jointly approached the Parliament in a political matter. But the action was taken in support of a feminist demand which had close connection with American ideas. And individually, all of them time and again joined the Liberal opposition in matters in which the United States had long before gained a symbolic value.

The dominant subject in creative writing of this kind was emigration, which represented the most intimate Norwegian contact across the ocean. Hardly in any other European nation is the theme of comparable literary importance; by its very bulk it demonstrates the extent and depth of the popular experience. Literary realism made the subject mandatory: emigration touched upon the life of a majority of Norwegians. Almost all the leading writers of the fifty-year period preceding World War I, as well as a host of the minor stars, used the motif.

From the point of view of this book, however, creative writing on emigration is in itself of limited relevance. Between 1865 and 1885, the subject did not create many outstanding literary works. More important, they were not concerned with the United States, but described Norwegians who, although they had lost contact with their natural milieu, still remained largely Norwegians. For obvious reasons, writers emphasized the more colorful private motives and conflicts behind emigration; America itself often became little more than a way out of personal crises or a background to them. For the same reason, writers naturally played on the traits of exoticism and adventure in the great movement. The dreary and also more typical everyday world would have to wait for description by the next generation of authors.

However, even the early literature of this type added to the image of America. Among the reasons for emigration, the writers unavoidably had to point to unfortunate conditions at home. The descriptions of the new land were dominated by a sense of victorious progress. Difficulties were surmounted, and the American dream proved to be more than a dream.

Such is hardly the stuff that great art is made of, but at least it offered the material for a literary monument of a different, but highly characteristic, kind. H. A. Foss emigrated in 1877 and never returned to Norway. His unpretentious little book *The Cotter's Son* (1889) became an unparalleled success, reprinted at least fifteen times in Norway and circulated even more widely in the United States. In its naïve form, the story confirmed the old idea of America as "the Utopia of the Common Man" and lifted up as its symbol the triumphant figure of the returning emigrant.

In circles with more sophisticated demands, the United States represented a good deal more. It was still the standard-bearer of ideas, a "vanguard of mankind," comparable to the image of America among the "philosophers" in the 1770s, to the dream of the Soviet Union among some European intellectuals in the 1930s, and to the similar vision of China in the 1970s. This image, too, was to be presented most powerfully by writers, of whom four are most important to this study. All of them were popular, and two of them knew America from personal experience.

The novelist Alexander L. Kielland (1849-1906) made his personal stand extremely clear: in a nation "where everything hated by reaction is being scolded as American," it became a habit to look up to and defend that country. He sometimes drove his point home jokingly. In one of his short stories, a youngster makes fun of a conservative assembly by reading aloud a terror story "from Illinois." He allows indignation to reach its peak before revealing that he has read a police report from good old Norway. Elsewhere, Kielland bluntly contrasted the solid experience of the emigrants and the "gang of denigrating bureaucrats." What moved him most personally, however, deeply attached as he was to his own home region, was the tragedy of emigration, the uprootedness, never to be fully compensated for by any success in the new land.

Much wider was the range of ideas in Henrik Ibsen's attitude and development. In his early poem on the murder of Abraham Lincoln, there was still a kind of somber hope on America's behalf. But the Civil War and its aftermath disturbed Ibsen deeply, as it did most thoughtful Europeans. In *Peer Gynt* (1867), nothing is left of his dream. It is the United States, equally the slaveholding South and the northern and western lands of business and gold digging, which have turned the protagonist into a person without backbone and standards. He sails toward his destruction under the Norwegian and American flags. When he approaches his doom, he symbolizes the rootless Norwegian emigrant who has squandered his life during two long stays in America.

Ibsen saw Norway itself in no different light. When in 1864 he went into many years' exile, it was because of that "Americanization" of the country which had disgusted Björnson a decade before. Why, in the course of the years that followed, Ibsen changed his mind completely, we don't know. Surely it was connected with his general radicalization, parallel to that of Björnson, but aiming less at external reforms than at the liberation of the individual soul. The result was his drama *The Pillars of Society* (1877), in which his general judgment is presented on the stage of a small Norwegian town. In the play, Ibsen pictures a depraved and hypocritical upper class, united in its condemnation of America with its "human trash" and "impudent radicals," and completely unaware of the fact that their social peers across the ocean are no less morally corrupt than they are themselves. Against this society, Ibsen raises the image of the "other America" reborn from Henrik Wergeland's dreams, a land filled with "the spirit of truth and liberty," and with "a larger sky," where the clouds move higher than at home and where people dare to be themselves. He presents his ideal in the figure of a returned emigrant modeled on Aasta Hansteen, representing not the orthodox and bigoted "Norwegian America," but the modern United States. It is not by mere chance that this free soul is a woman.

Kristofer Janson (1841-1917) lacked Ibsen's dimensions as a poet but was important in his own right. As a friend of Björnson and Christopher Bruun, he early became active in the "people's high schools." Those circles had just received fresh American impulses from Denmark. In the early 1870s a new Danish journal, *For Idea and Reality,* of which Björnson was coeditor, eagerly pointed to the growth in the United States of a broadly democratic civilization of the people along Grundtvig's lines, based on "the vigorous, proud and enlightened working class." In 1872 the editor was the first in Scandinavia to introduce Walt Whitman as a symbol of this development. Two years later, he translated *Democratic Vistas.* In spite of all the seamy sides of the modern United States, the editor maintained his faith in the regenerative power of the American nation, as did Whitman himself.

This American impact was also felt in Norway, as shown in reprints and appreciative reviews. The novelist Jonas Lie (1883-1908) called Whitman's poetry "a piece of hopeful green turf in this time of the millions." But to Kristofer Janson the impression was decisive in a more practical way. When in 1878 he had to leave his teaching position because of his freethinking, he went to the United States and spent twelve years there, working as an editor, lecturer, and Unitarian clergyman. He gathered his impressions in a well-balanced book in 1881.

He came to America with high hopes but soon had his eyes opened to other aspects of his new homeland. In his numerous novels he described the social contrasts and the reign of big money with a good deal of radicalism. He was particularly disturbed by uncontrolled mass immigration and feared a temporary relapse to a more authoritarian form of government. But he realistically judged the long-range prospects as hopeful: the American nation to him was "prone to exaggeration" but "spiritually healthy," with much common sense. Janson's faith in democracy was strengthened during his years in America. He saw a deeper motivation behind its political institutions: "This country intends to educate people through public confidence."

He also saw American literature in this light, and with a good deal of independence. The Boston school "moved in the old tracks"; Bret Harte and Mark Twain were "more distinctively American." But the central figure to him was Whitman, "the singer of democracy" and "the prophet of American realism."

Björnstjerne Björnson

When it comes to the general impact of their American impressions, none of these writers can, however, be compared to Björnson. Like no other Norwegian contemporary, he was at the center of his time, filled it with his boundless vitality, and was heard by everyone, adversaries and allies alike.

As we saw, he initially took a skeptical view of American developments and also of their influence in Norway. But from the 1860s onward he increasingly saw the country in the light of the liberal tradition. His collaboration with the America enthusiast Ole Bull was important, but even more so were his growing engagement in the political struggle on the side of the opposition and his convinced republicanism. He also changed his mind with regard to developing industrialization. To him, it was no longer an expression of materialism but a sign of America's "willpower and energy," worthy of imitation even in Norway.

A contributing factor was his discovery of Whitman's poetry, and his reading of *Democratic Vistas*. Whitman's great visions moved him "as if I were on the ocean, and saw the drifting icebergs announcing the arrival of spring." He began pointing to the United States as a political model. In his writings in the late 1870s, America appeared in various ways as a liberating force.

In 1880 Björnson was offered an opportunity to visit the United States. He happily accepted and spent eight months there.

He went "for his own personal development," not in order to produce a book. Nor was that necessary. He attracted a good deal of attention in America, and interviews and reports were amply reprinted in the press at home. A series of travel letters to his wife also were promptly published in the newspapers. They often caused heated debates. But, above all, they made extremely good reading because of their boyish exultation about the wonders of a new world, from the perfect ventilation system at Wellesley College and the "matchless" American kitchen stoves and mousetraps to his own dizzy balancing act between the sky and the East River across the half-finished Brooklyn Bridge.

In his feverish tourist activity, Björnson did not forget what he really came for. He carried in his mind an image of an ideal America, usable in his battles at home. But he also harbored many doubts and hesitations. He would confront his image of America with the realities and find out what to believe.

Björnson purposely limited his itinerary. He spent three months lecturing in the Norwegian settlements in the Middle West, but regarded this excursion as a parenthesis: the largely unassimilated immigrants could teach him little about America. His decisive impressions he gathered in the New England states. He stayed in Cambridge, in James Russell Lowell's vacant residence, Elmwood. He was surrounded by the most cultivated upper-class society, was received by men of prominence, and met personally or exchanged letters with all the literary worthies of the time. From this cultural center he also made excursions into New England folk life, visited historic shrines and factory districts, studied institutions and public functions, and even spoke at a Republican meeting.

Björnson's observations were varied, but to him they fell into a coherent pattern. He hastened to tell his readers at home that, largely speaking, his high hopes about America had not been disappointed. In New England he had found a truly democratic society where the political system functioned well, where universal suffrage proved a blessing, where apparently there was little class discrimination, and where there existed a general prosperity and sense of well-being. He found a keen intellectual life, religious tolerance, and a wide acceptance of human rights. To Björnson, it was all symbolized in the free position of American women. He wrote back from a feminist meeting in Boston: "I could hardly master my emotions. I felt as though I were in the future."

Critics at home pounced upon these rosy descriptions right away. They pointed out that New England was a not-too-typical part of the modern United States. They made fun of Björnson's touch of naïveté, his constant use of superlatives and easy jumping at conclusions. But such objections did not affect the essentials. In New England, traditional ways were still practiced. Björnson's reports were not all pulled out of thin air.

Nor was he blindly enchanted. He found that American tolerance had its limitations. He saw an icy greed behind friendly social relations and a touch of madness in American idealism. But he tried to balance things against one another: "both bad and good are larger here than at home." The political machine of the United States surely had many faults but served its purpose of activating the masses. There was much human depravation, but no other nation "castigates its culprits more mercilessly."

Björnson saw the limits of his own experience, but he firmly believed New England to be "the spiritual center" of the union. In studying a nation, it was wise "to begin with the most advanced states." Afterwards, there might be time to look for the exceptions and shortcomings.

What most deeply confirmed Björnson in his convictions was his impression of Americans as human beings. The main achievement of the United States, he wrote, was receiving "all the human slag from the mines of monarchical Europe," and extracting the precious metals. He was struck by this human quality time and again, from the men at political gatherings in Boston with their expression of "strength and health" to the labor women at Worcester with their "free, independent look." These qualities to him were reflected in American literature. Perhaps it had only two great names so far, Hawthorne and Whitman, but it had "a more loving view of human character than any literature I know."

Björnson's image of America was a vision born of one great experience. But it wasn't just a poet's dream. Upon his return he was always prepared to defend its essential rightness, even in great detail. The image played its part in the victorious battles at home for a full-fledged democracy, in which Björnson was one of the main protagonists.

His impressions continued to live in his writing, down to his final years. Again and again in his books, the ideas of the future were represented by individuals returned from the United States. Above all, this holds true in the field of education: by respecting the child, Americans had managed to develop those human values that, to Björnson, were the main historic contribution of American society.

Political Settlement, 1865-1885

The ideas and emotions seen in action above moved within different walks of life. But many of them pointed toward their ultimate political solution in Parliament. Here America and its traditions now proved to be an active power, as it had been in public discussions.

Old Sören Jaabæk was a member of Parliament all the way down to 1890, faithful in his devotion to "the country most beloved by mankind." He kept his hope that someday Norway was going to be "as free as is America." He was joined by a group of younger men with similar convictions; he was succeeded as their leader by Johan Sverdrup. On the right, there were men with no less clear-cut ideas about America, often backed by impressive knowledge.

These politicians had behind them the opinion of the people.

There was a widespread and ingrained Conservative distrust, often even a loathing, of the United States and everything that was associated with it in the popular mind. On the other side, there was a grass-roots goodwill, firmly based on the emigrant experience and Jaabæk's propaganda, and verbalized on a higher level by Björnson and the liberal press.

This sympathy also received a remarkable support from the emigrants themselves. The Norwegian settlers in the United States followed the growing political tension in Norway with keen interest. Björnson reported how, at midwestern gatherings in 1881, the mere mention of the name of Johan Sverdrup was greeted with resounding applause. There were numerous Liberal associations which collected money for him and sent him scrolls of greeting. One township was even named for him. When, during the action of impeachment in 1884, there was anxiety about a royal coup d'état, Norwegian-Americans collected money for the Liberal rifle clubs at home and even considered organizing a detachment of Norwegian veterans from the Civil War who were willing to fight the Swedish king if need be.

Sverdrup was grateful for the support and, in expressing his gratitude, referred to the joint heritage of 1776 and 1814. Actually, the practical results were minimal, but such political sentiments surely were reflected in many letters home and in the Norwegian-American press, which had propaganda value. "Each mail across the Atlantic," it was written in 1873, "brings health to liberty and self-government, poison to all their adversaries."

Looking at the factual American influence in Norwegian political day-to-day decisions between the American Civil War and the year 1884, expectations should not be too high. Needless to say, the real motive power normally was to be found in immediate Norwegian needs. The United States could only offer incentives or counterparts, forbidding or encouraging. It was far away, and European parallels were often more relevant. The details would also mean little to foreign readers today. Nevertheless, taken together, these scattered instances are of considerable interest. They evince a living tradition, much stronger than, for example, in neighboring Sweden, and on several occasions they played a real part.

In education, the organization of the elementary schools in the two countries now largely followed similar lines, and direct references became rare. But the situation was different when it came to the secondary schools. With their emphasis on the classical languages, they had in Norway become the symbol of the old bureaucracy and its cultural monopoly, and a main target of attack by democratic and radical modernism. The reformers aimed at a school in which Norwegian, German, and English would be the main languages and science fully recognized as a subject on a par with the humanities.

In this discussion, America played no direct part as a model. But both sides in the controversy referred to America occasionally as a representative, for good or bad, of that new civilization which was now forcing its way into the schools. The Conservatives pointed triumphantly to the alleged wildness of American educational institutions: there, children not yet confirmed regarded themselves as "American citizens," and it might happen that the teacher just was "killed on the spot."

Johan Sverdrup, as usual, placed the problem in a larger context. In 1869 he declared in Parliament that, in his view, the French language had been given a place in Norwegian schools which it had lost in the world. He continued:

> What is it that is rising so mightily in the West? It is a world power that is going to control everything in its development. English North America is going to gain a position of dominance in politics, in scholarship, in art, in technique. *Imperium Romanum* is going to be like a trifle compared to the empire that is now at its point of arrival. The European standard, so often evoked, in many ways is already decaying into rottenness. It will soon be broken asunder and replaced by another, which can be called European more rightfully.

In the continued discussion of the place of the classical languages, it was argued that even radical America stuck to the study of Latin. A speaker on the Liberal side retorted that the real link across the ocean was "the modern intellectual life which is now fighting for its place in the sun," not the possible fact that perhaps 1 percent of the two populations had read Sallust! In the final law of 1896, the teaching of the classical languages in the secondary schools was restricted more drastically in Norway than in any other European nation. English was now taught as a written as well as an oral language. It became a main subject for those majoring in language-history, a specialization which in the new century was to be chosen by half or more of all secondary school students. It was a written language even for those majoring in science.

Even in organization it was now demanded that higher education "serve our own time, not the past." This implied, among other things, a democratic progression from elementary school to the higher levels of education, as found in the United States. The law of 1896 meant a great step forward in this direction.

Emancipation of women simultaneously proved a burning political issue, prepared for by public debate. Education was bound to become the first battle line. The positive American arguments were provided mainly by Peter Voss. In the discussion in Parliament, it was maintained on the Conservative side that coeducation explained the unpleasant freedom of manners among American women and the lack of noble femininity in American culture. But other speakers on the right referred positively to the American experience. By this bipartisan support, the Norwegian secondary schools, and gradually also the university, were opened to women in the 1880s.

Another political aspect of emancipation was the economic position of married women. A government commission of 1875 built on American legislation to a considerable extent, but there was still a good deal of dissension, and the bill was passed only in part.

In a number of other matters of the most different kinds, from taxation and conscription to quack doctors and alcohol, American references came in more or less at random. Most important was financial policy, in particular the question of tariffs. But the subject remains extremely complicated. About 1870, liberalism in economic matters was generally accepted in Norway. At the same time, tariffs answered for almost half of the government incomes, and even important American mass products were now involved, such as petroleum, grain, and pork. Local interests in Norway were often so widely divergent that the political parties officially avoided the tariff issues and a joint policy proved impracticable. There was also interplay with the policy of the American government, which tried to further its own interests abroad while at the same time switching from its idolized hands-off policy to protectionism. But as before, the part of America in this intricate tug-of-war between regions, economic interests, and domestic and foreign goods has not yet been investigated, and answers have to be left to the future.

What aroused the deepest passions were the purely political issues, in particular Norway's future system of justice and government. Here the American impact often was manifest.

Not all seeds fell on fertile ground. Emigrants' letters early had spread republican ideas in Norway. So had Jaabæk's paper, and even more vigorously the enthusiasm of Björnstjerne Björnson. (When Björnson left for the New World, the Norwegian-Swedish king bitterly remarked that it would have been better if the poet had gone to the Other World.) But republicanism never was adopted as a program by the Liberal party. Opinion on the question remained divided.

Similarly, in spite of pressure from a highly competent group, the Conservative party never in earnest accepted as part of its plank the old ideas of imitating in Norway the American Senate with its restrictive authority. Only the American judicial review really gained a foothold in Norway. The Norwegian Supreme Court probably was the first one in Europe to imitate American practice quite consistently on this point. During the political battles of the 1880s, the Norwegian Conservatives extolled the judicial review with direct reference to the American model. After the nullification of the royal veto, the Norwegian Supreme Court, down to the interwar years, repeatedly tried to serve as a brake on progressive legislation, although much more cautiously than its American counterpart.

The American models had a much more important influence when the battle over the introduction of the jury system now approached its final showdown. The proposal was probably the most radical step toward democratization ever suggested in Norway. All through the history of the battle, the United States had been constantly referred to; but each time the government had succeeded in thwarting efforts to introduce the jury system. When, in 1862-1863, the proposal was made again, the old arguments were marshaled anew on both sides by the old fighters. Ueland called the reform "the keystone of the constitution." Schweigaard pointed to the shipwreck of youthful radicalism after "recent occurrences in the USA." But the bill was postponed, actually for more than twenty years.

The discussion did not abate, however, nor did the mobilization of arguments based on American precedent. After the Liberal victory of 1884, the question finally was ripe for decision. Before the debate in 1887, Parliament published a large collection of German statements on the jury system and a similar volume of testimonies from 200 American jurists. Both were used eagerly by both sides. But given the composition of Parliament, the passage of the reform was now a foregone conclusion.

The next great democratic plank had a more varied history. The extension of the vote for men was an old demand and soon was followed by similar demands on behalf of women. Time and again, American experiences and experiments were used both by the advocates of the two reforms and by their adversaries. On this point, there were closer models in Europe, however. Nor was there any unanimity in the matter. Even on the side of the opposition there was a growing wariness, created both by the new social developments and by the Paris Commune.

As a consequence. the extension of the vote was passed by steps only, under great resistance, and more slowly in Norway than in most European nations. Universal suffrage for men, in state and municipality, was not established by law before the years 1898 and 1901, and for women only in 1910 and 1913—in the latter year, unanimously. But on this point, at least, the example of the United States definitely had an effect. When in 1910 the leader of the Norwegian feminists was received by President Taft, she told him that the victory of Norwegian women would have been impossible without the great American pioneers.

Behind all these successive steps along progressive lines was the steadily growing determination of the people that final political power should ultimately rest, not with king and cabinet and their apparatus of administration, but with the elected representatives of the people. An important step forward in this direction was the introduction, in 1869, of annual sessions of Parliament. The final battle was opened with the proposal that cabinet members should meet in Parliament and be subject to its continuous control. This idea, of course, ran against American constitutional practice. We have already seen how the opposition on this point broke away from its transatlantic idol only slowly and step by step. When in 1872 the motion was passed for the first time, Sverdrup reminded his followers that the opposite procedure in the United States was understandable only because its president was elected by the people, as were its other officials, and could be impeached and removed from office at any time.

The resolution was vetoed; the same happened in 1874 and 1877. When in 1880 Parliament passed the motion again and it was vetoed for the fourth time, impeachment followed. After conviction, king and government yielded, and the first parliamentary government was appointed, with Johan Sverdrup as prime minister.

In strictly legal terms, in this historical process the United States had functioned largely as a negative example. But, considering the general trend of the reform and the many steps leading up to it, the Liberal spokesmen surely must have felt their action to be in accordance with basic ideas in American history and with the tradition which these ideas had created in Norway itself.

Although the victorious leaders did not refer to America's influence explicitly, their defeated adversaries did. The new chief of the Conservatives prophesied that Norway now was facing a wild dominance by one party and an ominous nepotism, as seen in America. The acrid Conservative ideologist Michael Birkeland wrote, when all was over, that "democracy is victorious and Americanization will proceed at a brisk pace." Then even Norway was going to live through what had been experienced on the other side of the ocean: a kakistocracy, or dominion of the scoundrels.

New Front Lines, 1885-1914

During the twenty years following the Civil War, America had gone through one of the darkest periods in its history. This fact had not prevented it from exerting an influence, and sometimes becoming an inspiration, in small and distant Norway, not only by its factual impact, but almost as much by its traditional image.

During the following period, from 1885 to World War I, the internal development of the United States in many ways brought it closer to Norwegian dreams about it. The revival of the liberal tradition manifested itself in political action. The United States of Woodrow Wilson's time differed greatly from that of James Garfield's. In Norway, too, domestic changes pointed toward new international relations. The everlasting frictions in the union with Sweden gradually led to the peaceful parting of the two nations. Internally, political democracy was no longer a subject of controversy. The economic transformation of society drew new lines of demarcation, political and social. Even the intellectual climate changed markedly.

Interest in America did not decrease thereby. Mass emigration continued, touching on ever wider circles. But those who left gradually met the New World with different attitudes. Popular self-government swiftly became matter-of-course at home; no more did America appear as a political idol or bogey. With the increasing closeness of economic relations, America's trade and tariff policy became more important than its ideology. So did its foreign policy. New internal cleavages made themselves felt in similar ways in both nations. In a translated article in 1891, James Bryce wrote that in the economic field and "also in the discontent," the Old World and the New now more and more began to resemble each other. Parallel tensions made themselves felt in cultural life.

At the same time, information became increasingly effective. American magazines did not yet penetrate to the Norwegian reading public, but a number of serious periodicals with an international horizon were started in Norway itself in the period; three of them are still in existence. A group of Norwegian publicists now more or less specialized in the study of the United States and wrote books based on considerable knowledge. The market still was too small for translation of the main works of foreign Americanists, but such works were read in the original. In 1890 one of the first people to borrow *The American Commonwealth* by James Bryce from the University Library was the first Conservative prime minister in power after the introduction of parliamentarism.

Knut Hamsun

The most important intermediaries during the period were, however, two individual Norwegian writers, who diametrically differed in their views.

At the close of the 1880s, the image of America was still dominated by the much-publicized ills of the "Gilded Age." To Europeans veering toward an artistic symbolism or mysticism or a Nietzschean worship of the overpowering individual, the mass civilization of industrialism was revolting and therefore contributed to a general rejection of America which was expressed drastically somewhat later by Oswald Spengler and Georges Duhamel.

These reactions were not unknown in Norway. One of the representatives of such ideas, the Italian Guiglielmo Ferrero, was read there already in the early 1890s. About the same time, a leading Norwegian intellectual translated an equally pessimistic book by the Frenchman Charles de Varigny. Similar opinions were expressed by the Norwegians themselves. A journalist, Anton B. Lange, emigrated to America in 1882 and five years later published a book, *America and the Americans,* which is probably the most sweeping and spiteful denunciation of everything American to come from a Norwegian pen.

The man who communicated such ideas to wider circles, and even outside of Norway, was the young Knut Hamsun (1859-1952), in the later years of his long life a writer of world fame; he was awarded the Nobel prize of literature in 1920.

Hamsun visited the United States first in 1882 and again in 1884; in all, he spent four years there. He was lent a helping hand at the start by Björnson and Kristofer Janson, but his own position was totally different from theirs. He arrived at the age of twenty-three, poor and unknown, with few ideas but with a burning ambition, and he decided to use America as a springboard for his own fame. He began writing about America right away and chose it as the subject of his first and sensational book, *From the Intellectual Life of Modern America* (1889).

During his American years, he had to fight his way through by doing odd jobs, as a construction worker and streetcar conductor in Chicago and as a farm hand, journalist, and occasional lecturer in the Middle West. His circle remained narrow geographically, and even more so socially and intellectually, a poor milieu of Norwegian immigrants. He had little curiosity beyond that, and his reading and knowledge were more than scanty. What he looked for and needed was not sober information about America but a foil for his own personality.

Travelers like Björnson and Janson were motivated by an active human sympathy. They came to America filled with dreams of a better society based on equality and directed toward high spiritual aims, and they were looking for a confirmation of their ideals. Hamsun saw with different eyes. He was a fanatical egotist, fascinated with the strange workings of his own mind and moved by a deep lyrical vitalism; he had little warmth to spare for his fellow beings. America, as he saw it, brought these tendencies into relief. He hated the conformist society of money and machines which had no use for the exquisite soul, but he had little sympathy for its victims. He despised the anonymous mob and hated democracy, an attitude which, fifty years later, let him praise Nazism and die excommunicated by his own nation.

The sector of America known to Hamsun lent itself brilliantly to a counter-image of his ideals and also served his immediate practical purpose. Initially, he too had praised American democracy with its "great, wonderful feeling of fellowship." But when he read the travel reports of Björnson and Janson, he soon discovered that his chance was to draw a picture as drastically different from theirs as possible. His book ends with the words "black sky." His leitmotif is to demonstrate that in all walks of life the American sky is invariably black.

The book, written in high spirits, is often amusing, with those bolts of thought and jokes of wording and that sparkle of style which were going to be typical of Hamsun. But the reader cannot always take it seriously as a factual report, and the author himself often doesn't. The observations frequently are trite, mixed up with gross blunders, and sometimes quite naïve. Literature is given much space; Hamsun praises American journalism, Poe, Hawthorne, Bret Harte, and, in particular, Mark Twain. But his judgment is curiously narrow: Mark Twain is "not a real poet, not a bit." Hamsun's long discussions of Emerson and Whitman are entertaining but superficial, written without artistic discretion. Rarely does he see his subject from the inside.

Particularly depressing is the continuous and ruthless generalization. Björnson too had an ax to grind, but most of the time he tried to distinguish between what he had himself seen and what came from other sources. Hamsun picked from his limited experience and reading all that was negative and, with colossal arrogance, declared it to be the entire truth. The only previous traveler whom he quoted extensively and often followed closely was a titled Briton, one of the most bigoted snobs of his kind.

Hamsun was not just after sensation. Beneath his negative reactions were also some of his best qualities—his unyielding independence and his love of all that was intimate and genuine, with roots in the soil. But in his book these values were overshadowed by his cold aestheticism, his vulgar downgrading of all social groups below himself—women, Indians, and Negroes ("African half-apes")—his eulogy of the aristocratic South, and his worship of an elite in his own image.

He may himself have felt these shortcomings quite early. In his old age he called the work "a sin of his youth" and would not have it reprinted. He also obviously had learned more in the United States—from the American journalists and orators, from Mark Twain's burlesques, perhaps even from Emerson and Whitman—than one would believe from reading the book.

More important, America itself appears again and again in Hamsun's own writing, down to his last years. The values and counter-values which he saw in America were reflected with increasing complexity in one book after another, and not only in marginal figures. His very image of America changed correspondingly. In the 1920s, finally, he praised American writing, art, and philosophy, the warming human qualities of the nation, and its genuine respect for decent work. The negative sides he now saw as part of the general confusion of Western man.

But his historical contribution in the field is the book of his youth. With its simple appeal to ingrained prejudice, it was read widely and was largely well received. In Sweden Hamsun molded the ideas about America of an entire literary generation, and not only there. As late as 1959 his chapters on American literature were published as a book in Germany. In Norway, too, there were repercussions from his judgment all the way down to the Nazi press in the occupation years, 1940 to 1945.

H. Tambs Lyche

Besides the consistent negativism described above there was also an opposite view. It sprang partly from the economic expansion of America, as we are soon going to see. But it also responded to needs in Europe outside the area of industry and business. Decadence and a fin-de-siècle mood called for contrasting reactions, a fresh vitality and an unsophisticated courage. These qualities, too, could be found in the United States.

In 1889, the year when Knut Hamsun's diatribe was published, a Norwegian translation appeared of the well-known work of two journalists (one French, one American), called *Jonathan and His Continent.* The book was written with much goodwill and emphasized the extent to which the American was "conscious of his intellectual and moral power." Two years later, James Bryce, in a translated article, similarly pointed to the latent force of the American "hopeful spirit" and "faith in the future of mankind."

The leading critic of the young Norwegian literary generation, Carl Nærup (1864-1931), who had visited the United States, branded Hamsun's book as ignorant and shameless and supported his own positive attitude by reviewing Paul Bourget's *Beyond the Ocean,* homage to the American belief in human willpower. In 1903 the leading Norwegian periodical printed a similar German article, which saw America's enthusiasm and spiritual health, so well demonstrated by Walt Whitman, as its distinguishing traits.

In the 1890s these ideas were expressed with a personal imprint and made functional in contemporary life with particular force by a Norwegian, H. Tambs Lyche (1857-1898), one of the most distinctive and sympathetic among transatlantic intermediaries.

Lyche was educated at a school of engineering and emigrated to the United States in 1880. He worked on railroads in the West and later also in the South, then entered a theological seminary, and for seven years served as a clergyman in the Unitarian Church, mostly in Massachusetts. He constantly sent letters to newspapers at home. In 1892 he moved back to Norway, in the following year founded the periodical *Kringsjaa* (Panorama), patterned on the British *Review of Reviews,* and ran it until his death in 1898. Under other editors, the publication lingered on until 1910.

As these facts may indicate, Tambs Lyche was an unusual man, possessing a keen intelligence and absorbed in all kinds of problems, technical, scientific, social, political, and literary. But basic to his personality was a pure and undogmatic Christian idealism: he would devote his powers to the building of a society guided by high moral principles. In this he felt himself to be in conscious contrast to his own contemporaries. Even in Norway the idealism of the 1890s often was combined with a bitter pessimism. Young writers turned away from Anglo-Saxon pragmatic philosophy to continental thinking of a more somber hue, often clearly anti-democratic. In Lyche's case, the main trend was a practical optimism, akin to an "enlightened" faith in progress: he was sure that democracy and education together would be able to create a better life for the common man. Like Björnson, he found that an ideal society of this type really existed in the America of his own day. It was his intention to tell the world about it, and he went to work systematically.

Lyche probably knew American intellectual history better than any other Norwegian of the period; his ancestors were the transcendentalists, and his hero was Emerson, in whom he recognized his own mixture of spiritualism and sober everyday practicality. These ideals to him were not something of the past. He saw them realized in the New England which was familiar to him from his own work as a clergyman. The entire society of Massachusetts in the 1890s fascinated him, as it had Björnson a decade before. Religion and moral life, developments in industry and agriculture, intellectual and cultural endeavors, the forms of human intercourse, and even the very landscape were, to him, suffused with the same sunny light of idealism.

Lyche described this New England several times, in a curious mixture of reality and dream. He was aware of many shortcomings, but he often painted his pictures without shadows: "Here is just one culture, one kind of breeding, and one education, one class, and one nation." Like Björnson, he was thrilled by the homes he saw and, even more, by the human types: "Never a face marked by servility, never an eye where the fire is extinguished. Here, light and happiness have founded their realm on earth."

Sometimes, such images are marked by a "will to believe" and by generalization. What distinguishes Lyche from Hamsun and, in part, also from Björnson is the fact that he knew so much more than they did about the rest of the United States. He had participated in general American life, social and cultural. He knew and liked metropolitan Chicago. He had worked both in the "wild" West and in a typical southern state like Georgia. Above all, he thoroughly understood the deep class conflicts which were increasingly dividing modern industrialized America. If, in his thinking, he always returned to New England, it was because to him this was the *real* America and essential to any deeper understanding.

Such ideas did not imply an escape from reality. Lyche did not look at modern America with the aristocratic superciliousness of his literary contemporaries. He was himself an engineer, intensely absorbed in technical progress; he burst into eulogies about the good American businessman. When he spoke of "obsolete and barbarous" Europe, he was largely thinking of its technical backwardness. But this, to him, had nothing to do with "materialism": he saw in American technical and economic progress the same creative vitality which he had met in New England, and he was sure that gradually it was going to be penetrated by the same spiritual values.

To find exaggeration and inconsistency in Lyche's image of America is an easy task. His reasoning often has a touch of the utopian. But it is all a reflection of his own general experience of the New World. He once wrote that "even health is infectious, as is disease." This feeling of spiritual health he carried home with him from the United States. There he had found the vindication of his own feeling of "Life's and the World's plasticity," pointing toward a new period in civilization: "Where America is today, we will find ourselves tomorrow."

This attitude was reflected in Lyche's periodical *Kringsjaa*. As long as he was in the editorial chair, America occupied by far the largest space in its pages. He cleared the ground in harsh polemics against the "superficial" conservative image of America, particularly that expressed by Hamsun, and the general complacency behind it. The fact was, he wrote, that "the life of the common man is more free, more bright, more complete in America than in Europe." The alleged shortcomings were more customary in Norway than in America. In his periodical, he wished to tell his readers how America really was and what they could learn from it.

Lyche did not fit the details into any preconceived scheme, but the whole publication showed, in his own words, "a certain spiritual unity." Before tuberculosis caught up with him, he brought out eleven bulky volumes. To many of the articles in them, which were borrowed from other periodicals, Lyche added his personal comments; there were also extensive articles of his own. He thus managed to present an amazingly many-sided picture of the United States, its history, and its present-day problems, within all fields of life.

The approach often was soberly analytical but always positive. His publication reached a larger audience than any other Norwegian periodical of the time. Under the new editors after Lyche's death, America receded into the background. But during the years from 1893 to 1898, his contribution had few parallels, even outside Norway, in the scope of his undertaking and the noble dedication of his endeavor.

Politics, Business, and Social Thought

Diverging opinions were also bound to appear in the Norwegian reaction to American day-to-day developments after the middle 1880s. Here, too, the change of atmosphere was striking. Still, there were remnants of the old right-left division. But purely political issues were now of much less interest to Norwegians. What, on the other hand, caused a sharp division of sentiment was the swiftly developing conflict between labor and capital.

The situation was dramatized in 1886 by the Haymarket affair in Chicago, where, after a massacre by the police, a bomb explosion, and a scandalous trial, four innocent anarchists were hanged as "inciters by word" of the deed. World reaction tells something about the image of America: Europe, which had noted with relative equanimity the summary execution of 20,000 Frenchmen during the Paris Commune, now was greatly agitated by the miscarriage of justice in Chicago. The incident created indignation in Norway also, as indicated by several Norwegian books, one of them published on both sides of the ocean.

At the same time, it is striking and significant that the non-socialist press in Norway, both Liberal and Conservative, still largely sided with the American establishment in the conflict. The reports expressed horror over the bombing and fear of socialism and revolution, but there was remarkably little sympathetic understanding toward the workers and their demands. In part, this attitude is explained by the one-sided news available.

Attitudes were soon going to be more complicated, however. One reason was the policy of the American government with regard to tariffs. American protectionism increasingly was felt as a threat to Norwegian trade and industry and called for strong reaction. In 1887 Henry George's big book *Protection and Free Trade* in favor of free trade was translated into Norwegian. It was praised even by the Conservatives, and it was also bound to raise serious doubts about American conditions in general. In 1889 the writer and politician Sigurd Ibsen (1859-1930), Henrik Ibsen's son, published a survey of the history of American protectionism, and in the same year he also bitterly denounced the social and economic powers behind it: "coal barons, railway magnates, millowners, monopolists and rings," commanded by the American Iron and Steel Association.

The American Homestead strike in 1892 was put down with military power. H. Tambs Lyche now wrote home with severe criticism of the employers. The reelection of Cleveland as president was generally applauded in the Norwegian press: Conservatives saw him as a free trader, Liberals as a reformer and opponent of big money. Lyche pointed to the beginning of the Populist movement, which he saw as the start of a peaceful revolution in the United States.

The Pullman strike in 1894 also was broken, this time by President Cleveland's own federal troops. Here, too, the bulk of the Norwegian press meekly accepted the official American version of the story. But some Liberal papers now used strong words about "the capitalist beasts of prey" and the "exaggerated system of monopoly." In 1896 Bryan's presidential campaign against McKinley created a clear division along party lines. Norwegian Conservatives saw Bryan as a danger to property while Liberals saw McKinley as the servant of Wall Street and Bryan as the enthusiastic spokesman of reform. Norwegian-American farmers wrote back to the newspapers at home in defense of the "Great Commoner," and Lyche supported them.

Therefore, the victories of the Republicans both in 1896 and 1900 were felt by many Norwegians as a serious step backwards. This feeling was connected with the appearance of American imperialism, both in the Caribbean and the Pacific. Norwegian aversion to it was bipartisan. American policy made away with many illusions in small and peace-loving Norway and called into question the very reliability of the United States in international matters.

But during the same years there were also more positive attitudes, not least on the right side of the political spectrum. By now, Norwegian Conservatives were no longer being harassed by continuous references to the blessings of American democracy. Instead, they were increasingly fascinated by the unbelievable expansion of American industry and business. They may have felt uneasy about the excesses of capitalism, but they were impressed by its tangible results, the effects of which were clearly felt even in Norway. The press in the 1890s teemed with articles, Norwegian and foreign, about economic and technical progress in the United States and its value as a model for imitation. H. Tambs Lyche was the enthusiastic herald of this message, too, in a special section of his periodical. The machines were going to emancipate the workers, he wrote, not enslave them. "With prosperity, we will have time to think." Even the pessimism of the *littérateurs* would then come to an end.

American business management now also came into the picture, turned into a kind of science by F. W. Taylor. (His nearest collaborator, C. G. L. Barth, was a Norwegian.) The new methods soon were widely discussed, imitated, and hailed as the inauguration of "a new era in the development of mankind." They were put into practice in the first and largest department store in the Norwegian capital. The same ideas also made themselves felt in agriculture and in many other fields.

Almost equally important was the impact of American business philosophy. By now, Benjamin Franklin had become old-fashioned. In 1904 Andrew Carnegie's *The Empire of Business* was translated into Norwegian. In 1912 the very gospel of the new movement and one of the greatest publishing successes in history, Elbert Hubbard's *A Message to Garcia,* appeared in Norwegian, followed by seven more editions and by his handbook of good salesmanship.

Part of the same story was the fresh public interest in biographies of American kings of business and finance, the Vanderbilts, Jay

Gould, Andrew Carnegie, E. H. Harriman, and J. P. Morgan. These worthies were described with some qualifications, but they fascinated Norwegians because of their Nietzschean dimensions and were pictured with a good deal of admiration, particularly in the Conservative press. The leading Norwegian business paper eulogized Gould's "invaluable merits under Darwin's law of the victory of the strong."

The most eloquent spokesman of such ideas was the Conservative politician and journalist Carl Joachim Hambro (1885-1964), eventually for many years president of the Norwegian Parliament. In 1908 he translated E. A. Bryant's *A New Self-Help,* a hymn of business optimism decorated with quotations from Emerson. Hambro continually used his paper as a mouthpiece for the same prostrate adoration.

On the Liberal side, there was a similar shift toward new fields of interest.

The old political tradition from the 1870s and 1880s had lost much of its relevance in Norway, but the Liberal press eagerly followed American reform movements, in particular the attempts to find an alternative to radical socialism. In 1897 H. Tambs Lyche pointed to Eugene Debs as the man of the future. What the Americans would prefer, he wrote, was not socialism but the present society balanced for the benefit of the workers, each industry being owned not by the government but by its own labor force.

There was a good deal of social legislation in the United States during the 1890s, and it was discussed carefully by the Norwegian Labor Commission. Similar specialized studies were carried out in the field of social statistics, prison and probation systems, and reform schools.

Two authors gave focus to social trends in America. Edward Bellamy did not leave much of a mark in Norway. He was translated both in Denmark and Sweden, where his thought played no small part in public discussion. A Norwegian edition of *Looking Backward* appeared in 1893 in Boston, but only 500 copies were sold. They probably never reached Norway, and the book was not translated there. Still, it was discussed quite extensively upon its appearance, and some articles by Bellamy were translated. But he does not seem to have made any lasting impression.

A far greater stir was caused by Henry George. We have seen how his work was used in various ways in Conservative propaganda, but it was the Liberals who were captivated by his basic idea, tax on unearned increment, as a possible peaceful solution to the social problem. In addition to his book on free trade, *Progress and Poverty* appeared in Norwegian in 1886, *Social Problems* in the same year, and fragments from his writings were printed widely. Henry George soon became a household name and the center of an extensive debate, even after 1900. A society for the promotion of his ideas was organized in 1908, and a Georgist periodical ran until 1927. This movement never became a political factor in Norway, however. It did not result in the formation of a separate party, as was the case in Denmark, and none of the existing parties incorporated George's proposals into their planks. Nevertheless, his thought may have influenced the practical development of the tax system. In literature, too, there were lasting impressions, in Björnson and, above all, in Arne Garborg.

The most important social impact on Norway in the period did not come from American individuals and their ideas but from the world situation. The fantastic economic growth of the United States more and more clearly made itself felt in the entire world of thinking, both on the socialist and the non-socialist sides. A striking example was the growth in Norway, from the 1890s onward, of the cooperative movement. The forms of its organization were borrowed from Great Britain, but America was a main factor in creating the needs in which the new idea had its roots.

Nobody wrote of this situation more vividly than the novelist Jonas Lie. In 1886 he described how big capital in the United States was creating hopeless conditions of economic life in Norway. "There moves a locomotive on the prairie, drawing a plough which makes a furrow one mile long. The steam threshing machine threshes bushels by the thousands a day, throwing them into the European market." The same thing was happening in all fields. The only way out for Norway was to adopt the spirit of the new times, "the strong idea of association." When Norwegian farmers in half a parish join in cultivating the soil as do the farmers on a big American farm, selling and buying in common and using the power and methods of big money, and when Norwegian shipowners and fishermen do the same, then they will no longer be "the servants of capital with wages paid by the day."

These ideas surely had implications far beyond the organization of the cooperative movement.

Theodore Roosevelt

This curious struggle of courage and diffidence, faith and distrust toward the United States was, from the turn of the century, focused in the figure of one American statesman.

In 1901 the murder of President McKinley—the third assassination of its kind in the course of little more than thirty years—made a gloomy impression in Norway. But the ascension to power of the vice president, Theodore Roosevelt, brought to the fore a man of picturesque and highly divergent qualities who made an impression abroad, even on the most different groups of opinion. Roosevelt's aggressive foreign policy was combined with his work for a system of arbitration treaties, a favorite plank of the Norwegian Liberal party. He was a social reformer, worked well with labor, and would check the capitalists, but he would not touch the economic system itself. His pleas for conservation and his muckraking were known in Norway; Upton Sinclair's *The Jungle,* translated into Norwegian in 1906, was accused of "socialist agitation" and caused a public debate. Roosevelt's trust-busting was no less sensational. The great bone of contention in Norwegian politics in the new century was the Liberal demand, against violent Conservative resistance, for a system of industrial concessions to check capital in its use of natural resources. Here, Roosevelt's policy was of direct relevance to the Norwegian situation.

Roosevelt became involved from a different angle when, in 1905, Norway broke its union with Sweden in a way which, from a legal point of view, was extremely unorthodox.

Agitation was considerable on the Swedish side, and war was a definite possibility. Thus, it was important for Norway to be recognized by the great powers as soon as possible. The Norwegian emissaries to the United States began working on American opinion. They were supported extensively and eagerly by the Norwegian-

Americans, who bombarded Washington with petitions for a speedy recognition. They even suggested the registration of Norwegian-American volunteers for a possible war with Sweden.

These actions had modest effect, however. Opinion was divided among the Norwegian-Americans themselves, and President Roosevelt delayed in making a decision. During the difficult negotiations between Norway and Sweden, it was suggested that they call Roosevelt in as a mediator, but it did not prove necessary. By a plebiscite, the Norwegians stuck to the monarchical form of government, to the disappointment of the Norwegian-Americans. But when more than 25 percent of the electorate voted for a republic, American sympathies surely played their part. When all was over, the United States was the first foreign power to establish diplomatic contacts with independent Norway.

Roosevelt's activity as an arbitrator in the Russo-Japanese war and his support of the International Court of Law at the Hague were behind his nomination in 1906 for the Nobel Peace prize, which is awarded by a committee appointed by the Norwegian Parliament. The consultant of the committee, the historian Halvdan Koht (1873-1965), was a great admirer of Roosevelt but could not accept him as a pacifist. Nevertheless, Roosevelt was granted the prize and was not a little idolized by the Norwegian public in that connection. His *Hero Tales* were published in translation together with J. A. Riis's biography. He was greeted as the symbol of American vitality and vigor.

In 1910 Roosevelt visited Norway to receive the prize. He was lionized by official Norway, and his stay was a resounding success. (Some less well considered remarks made by him about European politics were discreetly held back by the journalists.) But the range of opinion was apparent in the press: on the Liberal side, Roosevelt was praised as the undaunted reformer; to the right, he was the man to thwart American radicalism. Dissension came out in the open when, to the delight of the Liberals, Roosevelt publicly supported their efforts to curb capital, particularly in its use of Norwegian waterfalls.

Mainly because of President Roosevelt's activity, the Norwegian liberal press, up to the outbreak of World War I, saw steady progress in American internal reforms and perhaps also a more cautious foreign policy. The work of American pacifists was followed with interest; in 1906 Andrew Carnegie's St. Andrews address on peace and arbitration was translated into Norwegian by leaders in the movement. In 1912 the Nobel Peace prize was again granted to an American, Elihu Root, Theodore Roosevelt's former secretary of state, this time without dissent. The presidential Roosevelt-Wilson campaign in the same year strengthened the positive impression. To Norwegian observers, it was a decisive fact that both of the major candidates for the office ran on quite radical programs of social reform and, together with the Socialist Eugene Debs, polled more than three-fourths of the votes. The Conservative press found comfort in the fact that Woodrow Wilson's radicalism did not aim to change the economic system. The Liberals saw his election as the victory of progress against the trust-dominated right, "a great change that also will be felt across the ocean."

New Cultural Movements

The reborn confidence in America's possibilities and power of regeneration received fresh support from the 1890s onward in quite different directions.

All through the nineteenth century, the Norwegian press had printed laudatory articles about American public libraries. Toward 1900 these institutions developed technically in a way so as to make them the masters of the world. Through the contribution of two men, Norway became one of the earliest countries to take part in this growth. During his years in the United States, H. Tambs Lyche was fascinated even by this aspect of American progress and carried propaganda for the libraries in almost every issue of his periodical: "culture has to be democratized!" In 1896 he presented his plan for modernization, along American lines, of the largest public library in the Norwegian capital. After Lyche's death, the plan was realized by Haakon Nyhuus (1866-1913), who had his experience from the Newberry and Chicago public libraries. He was the first to introduce the new methods to Scandinavia and in 1902 carried through a similar reorganization of all Norwegian public libraries. No European nation has had as many students at American library schools as has Norway.

An even more far-reaching impulse from America reached Norwegian classrooms. There had long been interest among Norwegians in the organization of American schools. From the 1890s onward, the psychological and pedagogical aspects more and more came to the fore, furthered by the theory of evolution and its concern with the early phases of human development. In Norway, there was a new awareness both of the problems of adolescence and of school-age children, fostered by a new respect for the child as child. This was the time of the first Norwegian magazines and readers adapted to children's needs, and of the first creative writing about them.

Popular American literature in the field of education began being translated as early as the 1880s. The strongest impact came from "child-centered" psychological research, above all that of G. Stanley Hall. The details of this influence are hard to ascertain; there was much scholarly interaction at the time, particularly between the United States, Switzerland, and Germany, and much parallel development. But it is certain that, from the early 1890s, Norwegian educational journals began paying a good deal of attention to American psychology and pedagogy, "the keynote to the education of the future." Here, too, H. Tambs Lyche's periodical was pioneering.

Soon, these ideas raised a lively debate, further encouraged by the translation in 1906 of William James's *Talks to Teachers.* The subject penetrated into the teachers' colleges and into research; the first Norwegian psychologist to go to the United States (1916) worked with Stanley Hall. In 1903 came the first translation of the next American pioneer, John Dewey, with his slogan "learning by doing." There was a parallel interest in American work with abnormal children: the deaf and deaf-blind, mentally retarded, or neglected.

Important also were efforts in America to bring schools and adult education into closer contact with practical life. There was an early Norwegian interest in the Chautauqua movement, in Booker T. Washington's activity school, and in the general emphasis on "education for citizenship." Correspondence schools on the American pattern were introduced into Norway in 1914.

In the field of religion, there was now also a certain impact from

American movements of a more intellectual character. The church of the Unitarians was introduced in the 1890s by Kristofer Janson and H. Tambs Lyche, but it did not strike roots. The same holds true of other sects with loose ties to Christianity, such as Christian Science and spiritism. The philanthropic Odd Fellows had more of a following. "Christian Socialism" was introduced at the beginning of World War I with translations of W. Rauschenbusch and H. E. Fosdick. There was curiosity about other American movements, from mesmerism to the circle around *The Monist*; the first decade after 1900 saw a growing interest in the philosopher William James.

While women in their fight for emancipation were now gradually reaching most of their political goals, American assistance still was welcome. When in 1911 a well-known American woman minister was denied access to Norwegian pulpits, protests led to a softening of the rigid regulations. Two books by the famous feminist Charlotte Perkins Gilman (1905 and 1912) again caused vivid discussion. When her colleague Carrie Chapman Catt visited Norway in 1911, she was honored at a banquet, with the Prime Minister as the main speaker. At the same time, the most serious objections to Mrs. Gilman's books came from two women writers, one of them Sigrid Undset. The objections, however, no longer represented a protest against America but against the entire reformative direction òf modern feminism.

"Americanization"

After 1900 a more vulgar America was suddenly brought home to Norwegians through new media, with an immediate closeness never dreamed of before. In 1896 the first public movie performance took place in the United States. Only a few months later, "Edison's Kinetoscope" was demonstrated in the Norwegian capital, and the first movie theater opened there in 1904. By 1914 there were twenty-six theaters in the city, and in all Norway more than 150. The crowds frequenting them could only be compared to those at the contemporary meetings of the Moody-inspired revivalists. What those crowds saw was, to a considerable extent, an American product. The great war knocked out European film production. In 1915 half of the films shown in Norway were American, and the percentage was increasing.

Some of the productions were of high quality. But from the very beginning it was clear that the new medium and the capital behind it aimed primarily at the creation of an artificial world which appealed to the demand for daydreaming and entertainment of the industrialized masses that were now fast springing up everywhere. The America appearing in a great many of these films proved to have an immense and worldwide appeal. It was largely built on the Wild West, Buffalo Bill, and Nick Carter image that was already familiar from the popular mass literature. In Norway, publicly owned movie theaters and a cautious censorship soon were going to filter off the worst dregs among these products. But much of the flavor and atmosphere remained as part of the genre and strengthened the grip of the vulgar image of America on the popular mind.

Other forms of American social amusement too now began reaching distant Norway, above all the new "stepping" types of ballroom dance with their special music, not yet real jazz, but surely more bold and exciting than the polka and scottish which had so far represented the extreme abandon at small-town Norwegian dance schools. It was accompanied by a new and more risqué female type: the "Gibson girl" made her appearance even in Norway, both in the papers and on the screen.

The press, which transmitted much of this influence, itself began to show its impact. Some American details made their appearance early; the first interviews came in the 1870s. But Norwegian journalism was still cautious and well-bred. The "American revelling in crime and sex" of which the English now complained as yet was unknown in Norway. The journalistic style was gradually changing, however, with more news and less ideology and popular education. The material became less ponderous, presentation more varied, and language more lively, certainly not without the influence of the contemporary revolution in the American press.

Europeans of this generation were very aware of the "Americanization" that was thus looming. After 1900 the process sometimes was felt as an inescapable menace. Norwegian papers carried articles, both by foreigners and Norwegians, about the "invasion" of "Yankee-

ization" which was sliding slowly into European culture like a "dread-
ful negro cake walk." Sometimes these worries formed part of general doomsday visions, symbolized in the sinking in 1912 of the
liner *Titanic* with 1,500 passengers while on its maiden trip to America.
But even here, views were divergent in the extreme. Norwegian
newspapers at the same time carried articles which described "Americanization" as an unmixed blessing to European civilization, even
in the field of mores: it was apt to "bring out the best" on both sides
of the ocean.

What gave this discussion increasingly more substance was the
growing knowledge of new and different sides of American cultural life. American music was still largely represented by Stephen
Foster. While American pictorial art now was sometimes discussed
in the journal of the indefatigable H. Tambs Lyche, the palpable
influence of Whistler on outstanding Norwegian painters of the
time surely had little to do with America itself. But for the first
time there was now a real influence in Norwegian literary life from
American belles lettres. Transatlantic connections were becoming
more intimate. Publishing and the book trade were developing fast,
liberating themselves from Danish domination. General European
interest was reflected in translations in the periodicals. But, above
all, more Norwegians were now reading American books and writing about them. Some of these critics had themselves been to the
United States.

By far the most important agent was again H. Tambs Lyche. In
his letters home from America in the early 1890s, he was mainly
occupied with the New England literary schools and their "manli-
ness and power." Mark Twain was a writer for "coachmen and
stableboys." But later, when he discussed American literature extensively in his own periodical, the horizon had widened. He now
was more reserved toward the New Englanders and instead pointed
to "a new national period of literature" inaugurated by the more
realistic group of writers. He paid attention both to the "deeply
serious" Mark Twain and to minor figures in the "local color school."

The American to make the strongest impression on the younger
generation of Norwegian writers in the 1890s was, however, Edgar
Allan Poe. For obvious reasons, he did not much interest Lyche, but

he fascinated many of his contemporaries, as witnessed both in reading, translations, and essays. The judgments about Whitman, on the other hand, were ambiguous. Björnson's admiration in the 1870s was not followed up right away. On the contrary, there was a continuous negative reaction, even among first-rate critics, to Whitman's "non-poetry" and "cries in the jungle." Only Lyche sent home from the United States a long dissertation about this "poet of the future." Even Lyche declared him to be "no artist of the word." Nonetheless, he presented the first Norwegian version of one of Whitman's poems.

This new interest also was reflected in increased translation, which gradually took on respectable proportions through the entire range of literature. A more developed book trade now made it possible to profitably market popular contemporary American prose writers— decent, but to our eyes second-class—from James Lane Allen and Gertrude Atherton to F. R. Stockton and Lew Wallace, some of them represented by many titles. Of the completely innocuous Archibald Clavering Gunter, there were thirty-eight translated novels. At the same time, American children's books made their entrance in earnest, particularly those for city girls of the upper and middle classes, from Louisa M. Alcott to Frances H. Burnett (fifteen titles) and the Pollyanna books of Eleanor H. Porter.

Among more serious writers of the classical period, James Fenimore Cooper and Harriet Beecher Stowe still topped the list, joined at some distance by Poe. But the younger school was now coming: there were scattered works by Edward Eggleston, Hamlin Garland, Mary Wilkins Freeman, William Dean Howells, Mark Twain, Bret Harte, and Henry James. The naturalists at the turn of the century were represented by Upton Sinclair and Jack London.

The general popularity of these authors cannot be compared to that of some contemporary Europeans. But among active Norwegian writers, both in the 1890s and after 1900, there are numerous testimonies to the strong and lasting impression made by their American reading. In some cases, the United States still played a part in their showdown with the modern world, both in the spirit of Knut Hamsun and of H. Tambs Lyche, the great American men of letters being used both as arguments and guides, Emerson, Whitman, and Poe above all.

"Our Kinsfolk Overseas"

Besides literary and intellectual interplay, the most important contact, emigration, continued imperturbably until World War I. But the general changes from the 1890s onward gave it a new character.

The idea that the movement across the ocean was an irresistible phenomenon of nature was now gradually losing ground. Economic progress at home made the United States less attractive. The loss of labor force was increasingly felt. The wave of self-confidence accompanying the full independence gained in 1905 made continued emigration appear as a national disaster. The year 1908 saw the foundation of a Society for the Curtailment of Emigration. Initially, the organization concentrated its activity on counter-propaganda; later, it tried to open up new possibilities at home. This work showed no significant results with regard to emigration but, as a by-product, strengthened the feeling that "Norwegian America" was of national value and needed support. One sign of this interest was the opening, in 1913, of the Norwegian America Line, and another was the foundation, in 1907, of a worldwide Norsemen's Federation, in which the Norwegians in America were bound to play a dominant part.

One of the practical results of this attitude on the Norwegian side was an energetic effort to spread information about "our kinsfolk overseas," especially through books. As a climax, in 1914 the centenary of the Eidsvoll Constitution saw the publication of a five-volume work about Norway for use in Norwegian-American schools; the fifth volume was dedicated to the emigrant group itself and its life. These activities ran parallel to organized work in the United States for the maintenance of Norwegian culture. This work was largely planned by the writer Ole E. Rölvaag and based on the ideas of the Norwegian people's high schools. Rölvaag saw life in modern, urbanized America as impersonal and lacking in depth and intimacy. In contrast, he hoped that the Norwegian group, more organically grown from the soil, could make an important contribution to general American civilization.

Essential to this activity was the struggle to keep up interest in Norwegian language and literature and, at the same time, to emphasize the emigrants' Norwegian identity within English-speaking America (e.g., by official recognition of a Leiv Eiriksson day and by the erection of new Viking statues and the naming of parks, streets, and places for Norse heroes). More important was the raising of numerous monuments in the "Norwegian" states to cultural leaders of modern Norway and the efforts to encourage a general exchange of visitors across the ocean, often organized by the American Scandinavian Foundation. Repeatedly, large amounts of money were collected in the United States for good causes "at home." There was a Norwegian-American deputation to the coronation of King Haakon VII in 1906, and an emigrants' pavillion at the centenary exhibition in the Norwegian capital in 1914; the state of North Dakota erected a monument to Abraham Lincoln in one of the parks there.

The feeling of natural fellowship also found expression in creative writing. During these thirty years, almost fifty Norwegian authors took up the subject of emigration to the United States in more than one hundred books. To the Norwegian local-color school of writers this interest became almost mandatory: emigration by now was a regular phenomenon in practically all parts of the country. But there were significant changes in the writing itself.

Eulogies of the new land now no longer were needed and practically disappeared. A few authors tried to strengthen the feeling of national fellowship and others turned polemically against emigration itself; neither attitude was very important. As before, most of the books used America largely as a catalyst for Norwegian social and personal problems.

But the general soberness of the picture was new and this was bound to affect America's image in Norway. Pioneer times were over, the free soil taken. The bulk of the newcomers to the United States increasingly had to work as day laborers in the countryside or were absorbed by the big cities. In all milieus, the atmosphere darkened toward World War I; life often appeared as bleak in the immigrant novels, with a touch of unemployment and poverty, sometimes also of brutality. Above all, after 1890 the feeling of alienation and homesickness became a permanent feature in the writings about Norwegian emigrants. Even the returned Norwegian-American often had lost both his glamor and his message of ideas.

This sense of uprootedness was just a variant of that feeling of striking camp and moving on into the unknown that was general within contemporary Norwegian society itself. It is typical that the only great writer of the period to use emigration as a major motif in first-rate creation, Hans E. Kinck (1865-1926), saw the problem as universal and only loosely connected with the United States. To Kinck, the motives were of the soul, an eternal battle between "the whisper of the woods and the struggle for money," a mental discord that was driving "some to America, some to town" but was not to be healed anywhere.

The Norwegian writer who, at the turn of the century, expressed all these contrasts most comprehensively was Arne Garborg (1851-1924), the leading spokesman of the Norwegian farm population and at the same time a great cosmopolitan and a thorough skeptic and doubter, always urged on by his longing to believe.

In his youthful opposition, Garborg began by repudiating the idealized image of the land of liberty. This, he wrote after the Haymarket affair, is "plutocracy, the most rude, vulgar, plebeian of all power." He saw the spiritual effects of American life as did Hamsun: the United States was "big and coarse," with a "washed-out advertising soul," devoid of individuality.

But without qualms Garborg, under the influence of Ibsen and Björnson, also accepted other human values as American. People over there were "more natural and truthful," he wrote, "more themselves" than were the Norwegians. Even their humbug was "more fresh and honest." He felt that emigrants returned to Norway with healthier minds. Above all, Garborg was thrilled by Björnson's description of American working morale and American labor conditions. America was a country where the working man could even afford to read! Garborg threw an admiring glance back at old Benjamin Franklin.

For Garborg, these ideas were focused in the problem of emigration. From the 1890s onward, the population movement away from Norway became the great symbol of national decay, springing not from any psychological cleavage but from factual shortcomings of society. He tried to stop it by pointing to his negative image of America. But more important to him was the creation of better conditions and a new attitude at home, "an America within our own borders." In this attempt he hoped for the assistance of returning emigrants, who had "learnt to work and run risks." But, above all, he found the key to better social conditions in the writings of Henry

George. With surprise, he saw the great hope for the future of the Norwegian yeoman coming out of the very homeland of industrialism. He was actively engaged in the Georgist movement in his country and, in spite of all his doubts, clung to its basic ideas. More and more, these ideas came to be connected to his religious dreams about a return to the home grounds of his own childhood.

Toward the end of his life, Garborg found some comfort in American thinkers. He rejected Unitarianism and Russellism as equally shallow and hopeless. But William James's pragmatism appealed to him because of its open-minded tolerance, based on the idea that "what serves life, is good." James's philosophy was "a hotel corridor with doors to many rooms; and everywhere there are good people, good views of life." This, he wrote, is "a truly American philosophy, practical and straightforward, courageous and hearty."

Stronghold of Capitalism

Common to most of the views about America mentioned in this book so far was their bourgeois, non-socialist background.

This line of division should not be drawn too sharply. Many Liberals in Norway followed American socialism with theoretical sympathy, and a good many, particularly among the writers, occasionally called themselves socialists, from Björnson and Janson to Ibsen and Garborg. But the qualifications often were significant. Jonas Lie in the 1870s drew a distinction between overpopulated Central Europe, where a violent upheaval was regarded as possible, and England and America, where the workers followed a line of peaceful reform because they "believed their societies to rest on sound foundations." It was exactly the soundness of these foundations that was now increasingly being called into question even in America, in a way to be of influence even across the ocean.

The socialist movement started in Norway around 1850 by Marcus Thrane disappeared almost completely after his years in prison and departure for the United States. It was reborn out of the industrial expansion, simultaneously in Norway and America, and in both countries with considerable violence. The first attempts at organization in the 1870s proved futile. The leaders again left for the United

States, and the workers were canalized into non-socialist associations. Only toward the end of the century did the local Socialist unions, the Socialist press, the national Labor party, and the Federation of Labor develop; in 1903 the first five Socialists were elected to Parliament.

America played no part in the first futile efforts. It was believed that the situation over there was completely different "because of the higher wages and the more liberal constitution." If interest soon grew rapidly, it was due to Norwegian America. Immigrants soon began reading socialist newspapers—some of them edited by Marcus Thrane—and entered Norwegian or Scandinavian labor unions. Here, as everywhere, emigrants' letters became important links across the sea and often were printed in the Labor press at home. American socialists sent expressions of sympathy to Norway and collected money for fellow organizations there.

Liberal papers of the period also displayed a good deal of interest in American social conditions. But it was of decisive importance that some leading Norwegian Socialists in the late 1880s went to the United States themselves. In the group were two journalists, both of them later to become editors of the main Labor paper, *Social-Demokraten.* Their American reporting had a note of its own. Knut Hamsun's book, for instance, certainly was called one-sided and unfair. It was considered "excellent" when it came to social conditions. But he had completely overlooked the existence of an American Labor party, a dawn under the "black sky." The Norwegian Labor press literally teemed with American news, presenting not only glimpses of the seamy sides of American life but also encouraging reports about the solidarity and brilliant organization of the workers and their "exemplary strikes." The Norwegian discussion of labor protection and regulated working hours often referred to American examples: they showed that the struggle was not hopeless.

The Haymarket affair dramatized American conditions for the entire world, but it also raised certain problems for the Socialists. The incident had a clear connection with the formation in the 1890s of an anarchist movement, which appeared also in Norway. Such tendencies met with little sympathy among responsible Labor leaders, who were careful to dissociate themselves from this type of violence. Instead, the writers on the left pointed to the terrifying conditions behind the American outburst and the blatant injustice of the sentence. When protests proved useless and the convicted men were executed, the Labor press used the strongest words possible about their fate, printed their biographies, and accepted them among the heroes of the Norwegian movement. In 1897, the party arranged a commemorative festival in their honor.

Norwegian socialism also received an American impulse from the works of Edward Bellamy and Henry George. But here, gratitude was qualified. Bellamy had tried to build a real Socialist movement, and the Labor papers printed excerpts from his writing. But he was characterized as utopian: he did not see the roots of the social evils. More importance was attributed to Henry George and his "warm-hearted struggle." But the support he received among Norwegian Liberals pointed to his weakness: he would not place the means of production under public control but recommended "a miraculous cure" which would be acceptable even to the Conservatives.

General American politics, too, was judged with considerable independence by the Norwegian Labor press. *Social-Demokraten* caused indignation by declaring that the assassination of President McKinley surely was nothing to make such a fuss about. But the factors of real importance to Norwegian developments after the turn of the century were the internal differences within the American labor movement itself and dissensions about ways and means between the trade unions, which were cautious, nonpolitical, and fearful of anarchism, and younger groups of opposition, which believed that sometimes a more direct action might be necessary.

Similar contrasts were developing in contemporary Norway as well. For that reason, it came to be of importance that a second group of future leaders in the Norwegian labor movement spent years in the United States in the first decade after 1900. Some of them were later going to be active in the trade unions, others in the political battle. Two of them eventually became parliamentary leaders of the Labor party, one of them prime minister. But most influential were the two visits to America of Martin Tranmæl (1879-1967), the foremost agitator of the Norwegian movement in modern times.

Tranmæl supported himself in the United States as a wall painter, but he carefully studied American conditions and continually reported to newspapers in Norway. During his first stay, Tranmæl was deeply impressed by the brutality of the American class struggle and the open use of force by the establishment. He became convinced that a radical change was necessary. But he also was filled with doubts about the methods of the rigid and narrow American Federation of Labor. On his next visit, Tranmæl met the opposition and was present at the organization of the IWW (International Workers of the World). He was not captivated by the syndicalist ideology of the IWW: he wanted to put to use in the struggle all means of change, including the parliamentary vote. But the decisive factor had to be the open trade unions, with revolutionary mass action as their main weapon—strike, boycott, and sabotage if need be.

After his return to Norway, Tranmæl made these ideas a part of the mighty agitation which he directed at the new masses of workers created by the economic expansion which had occurred, above all, within the hydroelectric industry. The "opposition of 1911" made Tranmæl a major factor in the radicalization of the Norwegian labor movement that was going to last into the 1920s. Here his American experience was of palpable importance, as shown by direct references in the program. Even his optimism had an American background: in the United States, such ideas were now rapidly gaining ground, even outside the Socialist party.

The Labor press followed American developments with increased eagerness in the new century. In many ways, the picture was bound to be somber. The editor of *Social-Demokraten* in 1910 translated Jack London's *The Iron Heel*, with its warning against an American fascism organized by the trusts. There was also bitter resistance to American "Taylorism." But the main note of the reporting was a faith in reformative progress, a feeling that was also strong in America itself. The labor movement was growing in power. Even on the bourgeois side, a new attitude now apparently was on its way. A statement by Theodore Roosevelt on his political aims was quoted by the left as "pure socialism."

The main spokesman of this optimistic view was to be Halvdan Koht, a man of extraordinary vigor and diversity. He was one of the leading European historians of his time, with an output of almost 200 books and more than 3,600 articles. He also was a brilliant literary historian; his standard biography of Ibsen has appeared in two American editions. He was active in many areas of Norwegian political and cultural life, a leading figure in the labor movement, and from 1935 to 1941 the country's minister of foreign affairs. His personal experience of America came to have wide repercussions.

His serious studies of the United States began in Leipzig in the 1890s, under the guidance of early German Americanists. Never a dogmatic Marxist, Koht became absorbed in the interplay of general forces in the historical process and believed that they were bound to appear with unusual clarity in the United States. He visited America in 1908, the first Norwegian scholar to do so with the purpose of studying American civilization as a whole. He remained for a year.

He arrived in a mood of breathless expectancy. When he first walked up the streets of Manhattan, it seemed to him that the earth was rising beneath his feet: "I was looking into the future." Like Björnson, he paid relatively little attention to the Scandinavian sector of America, studying the entire country with scholarly thoroughness. He visited more than half of the states, saw the political and judicial systems in action, went to institutions of all kinds, observed the best society and the worst, acquainted himself with American literature and art, and met outstanding Americans, from Frederick Jackson Turner and Thorstein Veblen to Judge Oliver Wendell Holmes and Theodore Roosevelt himself. He "absorbed life through all the pores of body and soul."

He later put this solid and extensive knowledge to use in his scholarship. But no less he saw America with the eyes of an active politician. He had himself written the biography of Henrik Wergeland and edited the six-volume collection of Björnson's letters. Like these men, he carried in his mind an image of an ideal America, and he was eager to check it against reality.

The picture which he thus formulated, first in letters to his wife and later in numerous articles and books, was bound to differ widely from that of his predecessors. He saw the economic and social powers at work, both above and beneath the surface, much more clearly, and not only in New England. Above all, he studied the capitalist system, the all-pervading influence of big finance. He had no illusions about the strength of these powers and about the social injustice created and tolerated by them.

But he also saw the spokesmen of public reform and met the heads of the labor movement. In them all, he recognized the spirit of the great American tradition. His judgment often was harsh, but it did not affect his basic optimism. Time and again, he returned to the idea that the United States was "unfinished," at the beginning of its development. It was "plastic," in the words of H. Tambs Lyche. The very air in the United States seemed to Koht to be filled with strength and willpower. His study of America was "a study in youth."

In particular, he was struck by what he felt to be the unobtrusive radicalization of general American thought. Many socialist ideas about equality and justice, government regulation and public owner-ship were now imperceptibly being adopted, carried by "the strong sense in this nation of right and wrong." These views, with their balance of contrasts, to Koht were epitomized in the figure of Theo-dore Roosevelt. The President surely had many shortcomings, but he was "firm and tight from his internal strength." In this quality he was typical of his nation: "an immense underground spring of vigor, courage and faith."

Upon his return, Koht made these ideas widely known, in writing and lectures. As a professor, he became the founder of serious American studies in Norway, taught the subject repeatedly in uni-versity courses, and published weighty books about the United States, its history, and its culture. His entire activity was marked by that unbreakable confidence which was the main result of his first visit to America and was to be confirmed by visits that followed.

Koht regarded the presidential campaign in 1912 as "a battle for or against socialism" and saw the election of Woodrow Wilson as a victory: "an economic equalization is on its way, and will lay the foundation of a new national unity." In his *History of American Civilization* (1912), America, with its "generous enthusiasm," appeared to him as the expression of the best hopes of "Young Europe" and "was going to mold the world in its image."

§

CHAPTER 7

The War and Interwar Period 1914-1940

Close and Far Away

During World War I and the ensuing two decades of uncertain peace, the United States went through few basic changes internally, but its relationship to the world was deeply altered.

The entrance of America into the war in 1917 decided the outcome of the conflict, definitely demonstrating the country's position as a world power. President Woodrow Wilson's peace program gave the American military and industrial performance a touch of moralism which was felt as a continuation of the country's noblest traditions.

But the most immediate result was a new colossal expansion of American economic power. Between the years 1913 and 1948, American exports were multiplied five times. Less visible, but equally important, was the export of capital. By 1930 American loans and investments in Europe amounted to more than $5 billion, and they were steadily growing. There was a similar invasion of the world by American business management and methods of production; all over Western Europe in the 1920s, "Fordism" was praised as a panacea for social ills.

Technical progress further reduced the geographical distance between America and Europe; in the 1930s the first airplanes began crossing the Atlantic. Spiritual distance was reduced correspondingly by new mass media or by the explosive development of the old: movies and talkies, radio and records, the first comics, and the modern illustrated press. Through these channels, an "American way of life," or certain standardized forms of it, became matter-of-course to most Europeans, accompanied by the ever-present jazz. On a higher level, American scholarship suddenly became a world power, not only in technology but also in the pure sciences, medicine, and all forms of the social sciences. New American belles lettres, novels, plays, and poetry, took their place as a remarkable literary phenomenon of the period and gained a worldwide popularity. The change was marked, between 1920 and 1945, by three Nobel prizes in literature and twenty-one Nobel prizes in other fields.

In a way, the United States thus moved close to Europe to an extent not paralleled before. At the same time, developments on both sides of the ocean increased the distance between the two worlds.

The wave of reform which had lifted Wilson to the presidency in 1912 did not survive the war and its aftermath. The brutal economic powers that had dominated America after the Civil War reappeared in the 1920s in full force, creating a period of irresponsibility, corruption, and moral decay which ended in the crash of 1929 and the depression. Franklin D. Roosevelt revived the dwindling self-confidence of his nation and steered American society back on the road toward the welfare state, without discarding the economic system. But this inner regeneration ran parallel to a revival of complacent nationalism which tied the hands of the government and isolated the country from the world.

Europe at the same time created a new distance in its own way. The accumulated social tensions had burst into the open in the Russian Revolution of 1917. The general radicalization which that upheaval engendered everywhere also affected the attitude toward

America. The goodwill created by the great war changed to disappointment with American isolationism. The roaring twenties in the United States produced no new sympathy for the American political system; the execution of Sacco and Vanzetti in 1927 created an international aversion comparable only to that evoked by the Haymarket affair forty years before. The depression raised similar doubts about the economic system. The highly controversial New Deal made no deep impression in a Europe harassed by its own crises.

The bits of American civilization which reached the world in ever increasing quantities through the new mass media often were no more attractive. The society described by the brilliant young school of American writers sometimes appeared downright frightening. In vain Santayana reminded the world that "Americanism just means modernism, more pure in the USA than elsewhere." Two books in the 1920s, one British, one French, were called *The American Menace.* Aldous Huxley's apocalyptic visions against an American background were endorsed by outstanding thinkers in Western Europe.

In other regions, the United States became a part of organized political propaganda. Under Stalin, the official information service of the Soviet government gradually worked into the public opinion an image of America as the schematic example of capitalist exploitation and aggression behind a mask of democracy. Through the Communist party, the image took hold in other countries as well.

To the Fascist and Nazi regimes of Europe, the "enlightened" ideology of the eighteenth century was the mortal enemy with its democracy, humanity, and pacifism. The United States in many ways appeared as a spokesman of that tradition in the modern world. The Italian and Spanish dictators never managed to make their concepts hang together. But Hitler's ideologists elaborated in detail the image of an America discovered by "Aryan" Vikings, destroyed by the mixture of Negroes and other subhuman races, but now on its way to a new "Nordic" flowering under Teutonic leadership. An annual average of fifty books about America worked these ideas into the German people in preparation for the war to be let loose very soon. When it came, in 1939, the United States actually was involved from the very beginning, and its political neutrality was not going to last long.

Norway Neutral and Engaged

Because of the massive increase of material, the story from World War I onward can here be told only in outline. Even the material itself makes a summary account natural. More and more, Norwegian developments reflected a general European growth. Similarly, the United States predominantly became an exponent of universal trends. The time itself had something of the tentative: it was a real interval, when tensions were accumulating for the next explosion.

During World War I, Norwegian sympathies were not unambiguous. There was a skepticism toward all the great imperialistic powers. Germany still played a dominant part in Norwegian intellectual life and had the support of a small but vocal group of publicists, a good many of whom were later to hail Nazism. But France and the Anglo-Saxon powers had increased their influence steadily before the war, and the German attack on little Belgium probably decided the feelings of most Norwegians from the very beginning.

Neutral America initially played a minor part in this picture, although it had a role as supplier of war materials for the western powers. Norwegian pacifists put their faith in America for a postwar settlement, but day-to-day reactions were mixed. Henry Ford's peace expedition in 1915 made Norway its first stop, but it was characterized as "a joke" and received no real support.

What made the United States touch directly upon Norwegian interests was shipping. During the war, the neutrals experienced a boom without parallel in history. The Norwegian merchant marine played an important part in the transport drama across the Atlantic, which largely decided the war and at the same time carried to Norway itself the day-to-day supplies without which it could not exist. The United States automatically became an important factor in the Norwegian economy, and the consequences soon went far beyond that.

As early as 1914 the Nordic governments asked the United States to join an action to maintain "a free ocean" for the neutrals. The reply was in the negative. But in 1917 the German blockade and unlimited submarine warfare, with its heavy losses of Norwegian tonnage and lives, not only created a violent reaction against Germany among the Norwegians but also forced the United States to change its position. In February, the American government asked

Norway to join it in breaking diplomatic relations with Germany. This Norway refused to do. But when soon thereafter America gave up its neutrality and joined the Entente, the decision doubtless was greeted with satisfaction by most Norwegians. Again, as a century before, the United States was felt as an informal ally against a joint enemy.

But the situation soon proved to create new difficulties. So far, Norway had secured its supplies by separate treaties with the belligerents. Now the United States advocated a tougher policy toward the neutrals to force them into an active blockade of Germany. Norway could not easily yield to such demands, which were also used as propaganda against the Anglo-American powers with their allegedly plutocratic view of life.

The Norwegian government did everything to avert a crisis. The Prime Minister appealed to President Wilson personally and also tried to mobilize the support of Norwegian-American politicians. The Norwegian negotiators in Washington were headed by the famous explorer Fridtjof Nansen (1861-1930), who in 1905 had played a similar part as an emissary to Great Britain. It soon became clear that the American government would not be intransigent. President Wilson stated that he intended to treat Norway "very liberally" and even "draw a distinction between that country and other European neutrals." After protracted negotiations, Norway managed to keep up some of its vital exports to the Central Powers and to secure its own minimum supply of victuals.

In "Norwegian America," neutral Norway was regarded with little goodwill. But in the homeland the "Nansen treaty" strengthened sympathies toward the United States and, even more, Wilson's "fourteen points" in 1918, in which he had outlined his ideas about peace and the postwar world. At the conclusion of hostilities, there was a wave of confidence in Norway toward the American President. The goodwill was further strengthened by the publication in Norwegian of his collection of speeches, *The New Freedom,* with its radical, anti-capitalist program for America's internal policy. When, in 1919, the committee of the Norwegian Parliament awarded Wilson the Nobel Peace prize, the decision certainly was approved by an overwhelming majority of Norwegians.

The striking token of these sentiments was the periodical *Atlantis*

(1918-1925), with its warm expression of sympathies toward the United States. The American participation in the war was seen as an introductory step to the organization of a free transatlantic league of nations. Fridtjof Nansen himself, in an article called "American Idealism," saw American literature and intellectual life, from Emerson to Whitman and Lincoln, as the great testimony of that "spontaneous enthusiasm" for progress and that "unanemic health" which, from the days of Lafayette, America had carried back to Europe.

Bonds Breaking

The general goodwill toward America seemed to inaugurate a much closer interplay across the ocean after the war, but in some fields those hopes did not materialize.

In foreign policy, relations were excellent, as far as they went. During the negotiations in 1920 by which Norway gained supremacy over Spitzbergen (Svalbard), the United States supported the Norwegian claim. Also, the two nations in 1929 signed a mutual treaty of arbitration. But the most important field of contact was lacking since, from the very beginning, the United States was absent from the League of Nations in Geneva, which remained the focus of Norwegian international activity.

Another important link also weakened fatally when Norwegian emigration to America dwindled.

After World War I, the movement had regained its momentum. In 1923 around 16,000 Norwegians left the country for the United States. But beginning about the same time, a series of American laws drastically curtailed immigration, limiting the admission of "undesirables." Under these circumstances, it was flattering that little Norway finally was given an annual quota of 2,377, not much smaller than that allotted to the Soviet Union. But it was just a fraction of the figures of earlier years. The depression in the United States soon made emigration less attractive in itself. In the 1930s the annual average of Norwegian emigrants to America was less than one hundred. The movement had come to an end.

At the same time, it became increasingly difficult for immigrant groups in America to maintain their national identities. In isolationist America, the "hyphenated Americans" were no longer popular. The pressure from the English-speaking milieu increased steadily and was supported by advancing urbanization. The younger generation became assimilated ever more swiftly, and there was no longer any transfusion of fresh blood from home. A negative factor was also the difference between the rapidly changing language in Norway itself and the fossilized, bookish idiom used by the immigrants.

The group did not meekly yield to these difficulties. The national resistance movement among Americans of Norwegian descent was kept going with great energy all through the interwar period, and Norwegian studies were eagerly promoted on the academic level. Research in the history of emigration was carried out with model competence, to be climaxed by the contributions of Th. C. Blegen and Einar Haugen. There were parallel efforts in the homeland. A number of books were published in Norway about emigrated Norwegians, past and present. The first volume of Ingrid Semmingsen's history of emigration appeared in 1942 at the initiative of the Norsemen's Federation. The Norwegian-Americans still took part in national celebrations in Norway. The centenary of emigration in 1925 was commemorated by a speech by the President of the United States, by festivals in Norway, and by the dedication on both sides of the ocean of statues of the Civil War hero Colonel H. C. Heg.

But such official arrangements could not conceal the fact that "Norwegian America" now was fast becoming assimilated. The interest in the history of the movement was significant: both in Norway and in the United States, the time had come for a backward glance. The most important tie to Norway, a shared language, was cut off at the grass-roots: by 1930 Norwegian was hardly being taught anymore in midwestern elementary schools. Connections still were going to be kept alive in various forms far into the second postwar period, but Norwegian national characteristics began receding into the background of a life that, in its main features, was completely Americanized.

In Norway, the feeling of fellowship weakened correspondingly. Family ties were loosening fast. "Norwegian America" played a less active part in the cultural life of the homeland. The "kinsfolk behind the sea" were becoming distant relatives and parts of a distant past.

The more important direct contacts increasingly were being taken over by professional and social organizations outside "Norwegian America."

The most lasting contribution of the emigrant groups in the interwar period fell outside the area of everyday life, in the field of historical research and creative writing. Even the latter had a definite character of historical retrospection. Part of this writing showed a continuation of earlier trends, perhaps with an even stronger emphasis on the dreams at home and the homesickness of the emigrant, but these features were now more a part of tradition than of contemporary life.

Only in the work of Ole E. Rölvaag was emigration finally made the main subject of great literary art. He was both a Norwegian and an American, was published in both languages on both sides of the ocean, and gained fame even in the English-speaking United States. Although Rölvaag saw his own contemporaries with keen and realistic eyes, his pictures of real grandeur were those of the pioneer years; they were close in time and far away in reality. To the next generation of readers, even among Norwegian-Americans, Rölvaag's heroines and heroes of the prairie were soon going to appear as no less strange and distant than the team of oxen and the covered wagon.

New Bonds for Old

While "Norwegian America" swiftly receded into the background, the impact of "larger" America increased tremendously in Norway, partly in new fields.

Economic interplay was predominant. War was followed in Norway by a swift expansion in both industry and agriculture. The value of the national product was almost doubled in the interwar period. Norwegian shipping during the same years competed with Japan's for third place on the international tonnage list. The United States played a large part in this growth.

"Dollar imperialism" had not yet come into the picture. Some existing Norwegian firms were absorbed by American concerns, but there was little American money in new enterprises. Of foreign capital invested in Norwegian industry in the year 1939, only about

12 percent was American; almost 35 percent was French. But Norwegian imports and exports to the United States more than tripled during the interwar years, and the number of Norwegian ships calling at American ports doubled.

In the technical development of Norwegian industry, American proficiency certainly played no smaller part. Details are hard to get at. But the Norwegian National Technical College and research agencies within industry itself now surely kept abreast of day-to-day industrial developments in the United States. The same holds true of the organization and standardization of production.

Almost equally important was the impact of American business management. As early as 1929 the Association of Norwegian Industry published a translation of James H. Rand's handbook *The Road to Success*. The book probably was typical of the literature used both in the business schools and at the National School of Commerce (founded in 1936). The special field of modern advertising began its development in Norway during World War I and soon had its own network of organizations and schools, exhibits and professional papers, often closely patterned on American models.

In a wider perspective, the general attitude behind this impact was no less influential, its icy competitiveness camouflaged by business optimism and a semireligious "service" philosophy. The trend was international, but the American version was easily recognizable. In this context belong ten more or less heroic biographies of Edison, Rockefeller, Vanderbilt, and Ford, the last being accompanied by a bitingly polemic pamphlet and a translation of Upton Sinclair's no-more-friendly novel. The *Message to Garcia* still had its audience, "adapted to Norwegian conditions." So had Dale Carnegie's introduction to the noble art of winning friends in business and Frank Crane's articles (first printed as columns in many Norwegian newspapers and later in book form) about the stimulating value of competition as contrasted with the destructive qualities of socialism, the labor movement, the trade unions, and the Soviet Union. Rotary Clubs were introduced into Norway in 1922.

Numerous other manifestations of American everyday life also gradually began to penetrate to the average Norwegian as a result of the increased distribution of articles of consumption typical of interwar Europe. A good many American products were imported.

More often, they were imitated and produced locally and soon became common, regardless of their origin. Here the range was enormous, from plumbing and furnishing to transportation; probably half of the cars running in Norway in this period were American. Even more widely distributed were many American gadgets, foods, and beverages, the latter with their recipe and cocktail books. In clothing, ready-to-wear articles had arrived before the war; now the models often were American, including sweaters, pullovers, and college hats. New hair styles came as well—bob and shingle—together with a new popular emphasis on the beauty business and cosmetics, often imported from America directly or indirectly. In social life Ely Culbertson and puzzles made their entrance within these decades.

At the same time, in Norway as in all Europe, the public milieu was increasingly marked by the American entertainment business. The influence here was just one among many. But more often than not, an American style or taste made itself generally felt. The movies in Norway remained under the domination of Hollywood. In 1939, 62 percent of the films imported into Norway were American, some of them with sound and in color. From 1932, Walt Disney added a new genre to the list and was going to become no less popular in print. Much of the American impact reached Norway through these media, not least the impalpable but real "American atmosphere." When, in 1933, Oslo had its first series of hold-ups, Chicago-style, it was traced back to the influence of gangster films. A by-product was film literature in books and journals.

In music, jazz had its sudden breakthrough in Norway, as elsewhere, just after the war. Nobody could guess at the time what revolution in taste was thus inaugurated in connection with much deeper cultural upheavals. But even in Norway there were critics who judiciously gauged its importance. Among the broad public, the Hawaiian ukulele swiftly was replaced by the trombones and saxophones of New Orleans. At the same time, the syncopated rhythms caught on in dancing. During the war it was ragtime, after that foxtrot and quickstep, boston and charleston.

The breakthrough was supported by the new record industry, which was based on an American development of Edison's phonograph and swiftly revolutionized the musical world. American tunes now suddenly were brought to the ears of everybody. Soon after the war, singers such as Marion Anderson and Paul Robeson made spirituals dear to all Norwegian music lovers, together with other American artists and the round of American dance, pop, jazz, and symphony orchestras and American shows. More traditional American music, such as that of Edward MacDowell, also gradually penetrated. American musical life offered new opportunities to gifted Norwegians at the schools of music, at the opera, and in the concert hall, as exemplified by Kirsten Flagstad. The same took place in the realm of sports, where champions like Sonja Henie based their world careers on the United States.

In the interwar period, most of the serious cultural mass movements with an American background had long ago severed their immediate ties with the land of their origin and had become parts of Norwegian everyday life. In the religious field, there could still be some puffs of sensation about individual evangelists, such as Billy Sunday. But the only new organized movement of some consequence was the Oxford Group in the 1930s, later called Moral Rearmament. The group was largely distinguished by its use of the American revival technique in higher layers of society. After an initial agitation, it soon fizzled out, however. Its main result seems to have been a more personal religious life within the membership of the state church.

Less visible to the public, but much more important, was the American impact on scholarship. The United States now took its place beside the other great powers; in several areas it held a leading position, further strengthened by the influx of top-rate scholars from Nazi Germany. The great American foundations now began exerting their influence far beyond the borders of America, organizing research on a worldwide scale.

Norway saw a similar expansion of scholarship in more modest forms. Leading Norwegian scholars pointed to the American "research age" as a model and were impressed by the efficiency of its organization. Reciprocation took place in a special field when the chief librarian of Oslo University, Wilhelm Munthe, was asked by the American Library Association to appraise the development of the entire library system of the United States.

Most important were studies within individual fields of scholarship. Very often they were now facilitated or made possible by grants from American funds, fellowships, and work as assistants or visiting professors at universities. In many subjects, a period of study in the United States now came to be regarded as matter-of-course. An increasing number of American scholars also came to Norway, and an exchange of students was organized, particularly by the American Scandinavian Foundation.

Technology, science, and medicine still remained at the center of these activities, joined at some distance by agriculture, forestry, and horticulture. In all these fields, the United States often offered excellent working conditions to promising Norwegian scholars, who thus were lost to their homeland. Several Nobel prize winners belong in this category. Others returned to Norway and not infrequently were supported generously by American sources in their continued research at home. For instance, the Astrophysical Institute in Oslo and the Aurora Borealis Observatory in Tromsö both were built by the Rockefeller Foundation for Norwegian scholars.

The social sciences and the humanities still were in the background. But American philosophy now was discovered in earnest, particularly that of William James, whose *Religious Experience* was translated and had a noticeable impact. The first Norwegian doctoral thesis on a subject from American intellectual history was a dissertation on Josiah Royce (1934).

The most influential subject aside from science was psychology. In the course of a few years, its practical application along American lines gave it a totally new place in Norwegian society. There were early influences in psychotechnique and testing. But the subjects with the widest impact were mental hygiene and school psychology, both introduced in the 1930s and soon followed up by vivid popularization in books and journals. Among the new influences was also that of behaviorism. The entire pedagogical debate from the 1920s onward centered around the Norwegian section of New Education Fellowship and was deeply influenced both by John Dewey and by American school experiments, such as those of Dalton, Gary, and Winnetka. New plans for the Norwegian elementary schools issued in 1939 showed the impact of these ideas. So did the pedagogical discussion in the secondary schools. The change of atmosphere was indicated by the fact that, between the two world wars, the Norwegian Academy of Science elected twenty-two American members—fifteen scientists, four physicians, two economists, and one Old Norse philologist.

Even among the general public, interest in the Western World increased considerably in Norway. Curiosity could now be satisfied much more easily than before. In part, this change was connected with a more general shift: with the ascent of Nazism, Germany swiftly lost its former dominant position in Norway's intellectual life. Symbolically, in 1936 English was introduced as the first foreign language in the elementary schools of larger cities. But the schools gradually became less important as sources of information than other media such as the movies and, above all, the radio. From its organization in 1925, the Norwegian State Broadcasting system set itself a clearly pedagogical objective and gradually made news about America an important part of its service.

The Norwegian newspapers from 1918 organized their international connections more effectively and also increasingly developed their own presentation in a more popular direction, geared to the new tempo. The first Norwegian School of Journalism was founded on American models in 1919. But the strongest American influences on journalism came partly by direct imitation, partly through Danish intermediaries: a layout with great headlines and more variation and the use of pictures, features, human-interest material, and shorter articles, all written clearly and tersely for busy readers.

With the growing strength of Norwegian publishing, more solid and connected information about America was now presented. During the interwar years, more than a dozen travel books and commentaries about America appeared in print, most of them written by Norwegians and highly varied in their points of view. In addition, C. J. Hambro wrote four books about various aspects of American civilization. He was joined by other popularizers of American history and geography. In the university, there was frequent teaching of American history, both by Halvdan Koht and his younger colleagues. America's place in the world was discussed competently in the journal *Internasjonal politikk.*

An American Self-Portrait

A striking feature of the 1920s and 1930s was the Norwegian discovery, on a large scale, of American contemporary writing. The literature of the Nick Carter type now receded to the back streets, and the Indians appeared thrilling to children only. Instead, there was a vulgar literature of a different kind: the weekly illustrated magazines began their mushroom growth in Norway, as did their counterparts across the Atlantic. They have constituted a major part of the reading matter among broad layers of the population up to the present day. In Norway, as everywhere, love stories made up much of the content. They normally had a happy ending, were extremely decent, were flat like the prairie, and were set in an urban consumers' society which was accepted as matter-of-course. A great percentage of them, in Norway as everywhere, were of American origin.

"Better" literature addressed a smaller audience, but that audience was growing, and so was the offering.

Norwegian critics paved the way, above all the librarian and journalist Arne Kildal (1885-1972), who early discussed American literature from its beginnings to the present, particularly in his book *The Voice of America* (1935). Other critics competently surveyed American poetry from Whitman to E. A. Robinson and Robert Frost, with translated samples. But it was the translation of belles lettres in book form, particularly novels, which was typical of the period. In the early 1920s, the American translations numbered less than one-third of the translations from English published in Norway, but in the following decade almost one-half.

Initially, after the war, Upton Sinclair represented the American novel almost alone. The change was brought on by the novelist and critic Sigurd Hoel (1890-1960), reader to the Gyldendal publishing house. In Paris in 1926 he discovered Hemingway and, in 1929, initiated "The Yellow Series" of new novels, which opened with *The Sun Also Rises* and ran to a total of more than one hundred volumes. About half of the titles appeared before 1940, and more than one-third of those were American, representing most of the new, great names. The undertaking was a pioneer job, not only in

Norway. A number of authors had their first European translations in the "Yellow Series," among them the Americans Erskine Caldwell and William Faulkner.

The series also served as a stimulant to other publishers, who added a number of good names to the list and gradually also filled the worst gaps among the great neglected novels of the previous generation of American writers. Besides, there was also an impressive number of translations of books which presumably sold better. Sometimes, literary and economic expectations coincided; during these twenty years, Jack London had thirty-three books translated. There was also a generous sampling of authors who were less ambitious but no less typical of their American times, from Harvey Allen and Margaret Mitchell to Edna Ferber, Elmer Rice, and many lesser authors. Detective stories and books for young girls and children now defied counting.

In the course of a few years, a surprisingly comprehensive cross-section of American interwar literature was thus made available to Norwegian readers. The more serious translations appeared in quite small printings, most of no mòre than 2,000 copies. This did not prevent a wide circulation; a good many Norwegians now also read books in English. In 1938 the largest Norwegian public library reported that the Americans had the largest loan among the English-writing authors.

In the theater the same thing happened. Eugene O'Neill was first played in Oslo in 1924 (*Anna Christie*), and during the following two decades eight more of his plays were performed in Norway. *Ah Wilderness* had its first European performance in Oslo; the performance of *Desire Under the Elms* was called the foremost Norwegian theatrical event of the century. A number of other leading American dramatists also were played in Norway in the period, as well as many of the less important.

There was serious critical appraisal of this current literary production. The university still played no part in the activity; as yet, there was no real academic study of American literature. But newspapers and periodicals devoted a good deal of space to competent judgment both of books and plays; so did literary essays. Of special importance were the volumes containing Sigurd Hoel's introductions to the novels in the "Yellow Series."

The real impact of all these works and judgments would be the subject of a separate book. Neither in range nor depth can it be compared to similar influences in the past, such as that of German romanticism or French naturalism. But there is no doubt about its importance. American writers were instrumental in molding a new taste and giving expression to a definite change of atmosphere. Their influence on Norwegian writers often was palpable in subject matter, presentation, and language, and sometimes also in the very scale of values.

Toward Crisis

In the interwar period, America was no less than before the subject of evaluation, discussion, and controversy in Norway. Here, the natural dividing line is the international crisis beginning around 1930. A real analysis of opinion would have to take into account the immense mass of newspapers. In this chapter, it is possible only to point out some important attitudes, reflected mainly in books and periodicals.

The American abstention from the League of Nations evoked mixed reactions in Norway. There was widespread skepticism toward the peace treaty of Versailles. The Socialists called the League "the Holy Alliance of counter-revolution" which Norway certainly shouldn't join. But also on the non-socialist side it was maintained that, without the participation of Germany and the Soviet Union, the League was a "victors' club" and Norway, "in the spirit of Eidsvoll," ought to follow the American example.

Nevertheless, the great majority of the members of Parliament voted for Norway's entrance into the League, and the new organization was initially met with an almost moving confidence on the part of the Norwegian people. The United States, on the other hand, avoided being involved in the increasing disappointment about the League. When, later in the postwar years, Fridtjof Nansen took up his magnificent work for the millions of refugees and the starving Russians and was met with callousness and cynicism at Geneva, he raised impressive funds himself with American assistance. Nansen called the relief action organized by Herbert Hoover "a marvellous page in the history of philanthropy.'' For his own contribution, Nansen was given the Nobel Peace prize in 1922.

American initiatives along the same line, such as the disarmament conference in Washington in 1921, also aroused sympathy in Norway. Additional Nobel prizes granted to Americans (Charles Dawes, 1925; F. B. Kellogg, 1929; Jane Addams and N. M. Butler, 1931) were recognitions of an American contribution in the same direction. But there were also many doubts, particularly with regard to the American reparations policy. As the advance of the totalitarian powers in Europe became ever more threatening, there was an increasing bitterness toward "sterile and negative" American isolationism.

This feeling of distance was not due just to American policy, however. As a matter of fact, all through the 1920s and early 1930s, America and its problems were bound to appear as quite irrelevant to many of the burning questions in contemporary Norway. This holds true of the great national issues with their endless debates, among them the internal language controversy, the conflict with Denmark about Greenland, the question of alcohol prohibition, and the ensuing diplomatic troubles with the wine-producing countries. There was the same irrelevance when it came to economic and social questions, which were of even greater importance.

The swift expansion of Norwegian economy in the interwar period was not painless. It was accompanied by severe maladjustments, aggravated by successive international recessions. The situation was difficult in the countryside; in the manufacturing towns, strikes were not without violence. The labor movement was radicalized; from 1919 to 1923, it joined the Communist International, until the meddling of the commisars became unbearable. Threats of revolutionary measures were more frank in Norway at the time than in most countries. On the extreme right there were anti-parliamentarian movements. Among the leaders was Vidkun Quisling, whose ideas were parallel to those of Fascism and Nazism. Here the United States had little to contribute. There was certainly a general interest as before, but events across the Atlantic were far less sensational than the turmoil in Europe itself and its repercussions in Africa and in the League.

On the non-socialist side, the ideological battles about America had died down by now. The American presidents in the 1920s did not appear as political heroes to anybody, nor did American social developments call for any enthusiasm. The worship of American business still had its active spokesman in C. J. Hambro. After the war, he continued his aggressive praise of American "help-yourself philosophy" as contrasted with Norwegian "social whimpering." There were also glimpses of more advanced capitalist attitudes; in 1919 the pleas of John D. Rockefeller, Jr., for representation in industry appeared in Norwegian translation. But in the "roaring twenties" such positive features were swiftly overshadowed by more exciting American news about political corruption, social and racial oppression, gangsterism, cultural density, and moral disintegration which, in 1934, "had filled the world press with loathsome sensations for years." Toward the end of the decade, depression was going to change the picture drastically.

To middle-of-the-road Norwegians of the 1920s, news of America still had something of the remote, extraneous, and slightly unreal, like greetings from a different world. The situation was about the same within the more extreme groups in Norwegian politics.

Antidemocratic voices of a more traditional kind still were raised occasionally in the wake of the war, with the United States as a negative example. But such instances were rare. Even in the confused ideology of Vidkun Quisling, America had little reality. He occasionally touched upon American imperialism and the power of the executive in the United States, but he was more thrilled by fantastic speculations about the "Nordic" foundation of American civilization and a possible transatlantic "Nordic Union" which would absorb the Norwegian population surplus.

To the leaders of Labor, the United States was a world of facts. It was brought closer when in 1918 the radical leader Erling Falk (1887-1940) returned to Norway after eleven years there. He was a man of unusual intellectual powers and an almost magic personal charm. He had behind him a brilliant career in American business, during which he had been very impressed with the IWW and its syndicalist ideas. He went home in order to revolutionize Norway in strong opposition to the more sedate wing of the Labor party. As his political instrument he organized the communist student group

Mot Dag (Dawn), which, in the interwar period, wielded considerable power in Norwegian public discussion through its journal of
the same name.

In Labor circles, the social tensions in contemporary America
were followed with particular concern: the "red scare" in the 1920s,
the brutal suppression of the unions and the labor movement, and
the simultaneous foreign expansion of American capital. The earlier
optimism with regard to American developments now had a rough
time of it. Even Halvdan Koht wrote in 1926, at the commemoration
of the American Revolution, that he was terrified by the present lack
of freedom in the country: "We always have to prepare for new
battles, a new revolution."

Such somber views were sadly confirmed by the trial of Sacco
and Vanzetti and their execution in 1927 after seven years in prison.
The case caused deep indignation all over Europe and no less in
Norway, particularly in Labor circles. The many speeches and edi-
torials in the party press often expressed an undisguised hatred of
capitalist America, which had committed "one of the most ghastly
crimes in world history"; all confidence in its honesty was lost. For
the first time, the American legation in Oslo had to be guarded by
police. The leading Labor paper printed the news of the execution
under the Biblical heading, "It Is Finished," and the crowds at the
commemorative meetings dedicated themselves to a continued
fight against "this society of vileness." The Conservative press
pointed to a lack of proportion in these protests, as compared to
Labor reactions toward the Soviet Union, but the Socialist attitude
was undeniably the more perceptive: America no longer was seen as
something unique but as an expression of general social forces which
were active on both sides of the Atlantic.

Such incidents could not conceal the fact that, ordinarily, the
United States had little to do with day-to-day problems in Norwegian
politics. The main concerns of the Socialists in the 1920s were their
endless haggling with Moscow, and the ensuing cleavage within the
Labor movement itself. The only American impact in that battle
may have been a heritage from American syndicalists, their radicalism and their rebelliousness against all kinds of autocracy. But at
best the influence was peripheral. The journal *Mot Dag* published

frequent and unpleasant reports about American conditions in the 1920s, but without much commitment.

In the general debate of cultural trends it was different. Even here, America was not at the center, but there was a definite concern.

The strongest strain was the least palpable: that "modernism" and moral radicalism which the United States now came to represent. These impressions had many sources; as an example one may mention the translation of Judge Ben B. Lindsey's plea for "companionate marriage," which appeared in 1928 and caused an excited discussion. But the main image of American mores doubtless was based on the new American novels, above all those of Hemingway. In a special manner, the Americans were felt as typical of the times; Sigurd Hoel in 1929 wondered whether Hemingway did not "correspond to something new in the modern reality." A young Norwegian in 1933 spoke of the older generation that hadn't grown up with "movies, radio, air travelling, cars, Freud, Watson, Huxley and Hemingway."

The gospel of the new faith, or lack of such, was *The Sun Also Rises*. Neutral Norway had offered its youth no personal experience similar to that of Hemingway's heroes. Still, the very style of life in the book made a deep impression on an entire Norwegian generation, as well as its disillusionment, the revolt against established standards of conduct, and the sober honesty beneath the cynicism.

The Norwegian conservative reaction to these currents fitted into a general European aversion in the 1920s to this new brand of Americanism. In reading today Georges Duhamel's 1930 diatribe against America, one is struck by the fact that a good many of the features loathed most violently by the author are now felt as obvious parts of modern life and not as particularly "American." Notwithstanding, the Norwegian reaction is not devoid of interest. Often it was based on American self-criticism, in particular that expressed by H. L. Mencken.

The most eccentric view came from an intellectual freelancer and outsider, Erling Winsnes (1893-1935), who never was willing to adapt himself to any regular milieu. His kinship with Nazism was obvious. His original contribution was his "law of danger": like Arnold Toynbee, he saw physical challenge as the decisive factor in the life of nations. In accordance with this idea, Winsnes described the United States as aging, mechanized, taylorized, and doomed in its hunt for softness and physical comfort.

A more curious disgust appeared in the Norwegian reaction to Marc Connelly's Negro play *Green Pastures,* in which the Lord appeared on the stage. In 1932 it was forbidden as blasphemous by a vote in the Norwegian Parliament. But the critics were disturbed less by such exotic excesses than by the average American youth of the time as he was described in creative literature. There was a good deal of discussion of contemporary Norwegian youngsters as compared to their counterparts overseas. Behind such worries was the fear of an increasing conformism and mechanization. Two French books, by Lucien Romier and André Siegfried, both from the year 1927, were reviewed in Norway with deep pessimism: here the worst forebodings of Tocqueville were vindicated. The most that Europe now could hope for was to throw "a small element of the unpredictable" into this metallic and monotonous world.

The most connected and explicit pessimism was found in a small group of writers held together by their Christian and humanistic view of life. In their manifesto, *The Dividing Line* (1929), Irving Babbitt was extolled as the great critic of "arrogant progress" and the worship of quantity, and Mencken as the castigator of American "standardized man." But this group also was willing to recognize "another America." Babbitt and Mencken, after all, stood for the traditions of humanism. There were other American intellectuals who showed a similar independence of thought, who never went to the movies or read the *Saturday Evening Post,* and had a pitying laugh for Elbert Hubbard and Frank Crane: "perhaps they represent *real* America." Among Norwegian publicists who really knew the United States, such as Arne Kildal, there existed a clear understanding of these built-in contrasts in American life and there was an attempt at a balanced judgment.

Even more important was the growing realization, parallel to that found among the Socialists, that America very soon was not going to appear as "American" anymore, but just as one variation of a world civilization. Sometimes, the simplification went one step further, identifying the American and Russian brands of standardization—"Asia and America united by Henry Ford"—while Europe was left out. But more fruitful was the admission that European (and Norwegian) civilization was now being "Americanized," of its own free will. Norwegian industry was being standardized according to its best ability. Norwegian politics perhaps was not so basically different from that of America. The youth on both sides of the ocean might have much in common, willingly devouring banal films, cheap magazines, *Pollyanna,* and even Frank Crane in spite of their "overwhelming stupidity."

The most remarkable expression of such ideas was found in the only large-scale Norwegian work in cultural philosophy of the period, Georg Brochmann's two-volume *Man and The Machine* (1937). In these "snapshots of the world at the entrance to a new age," the author competently analyzed the entire technical world civilization, field by field. The United States was included, but the American material was not predominant, and the United States was never used as a scapegoat for the general development. On the contrary, the author demonstrated how many of American national characteristics had already been neutralized by the formation of a truly global form of life.

Bulwark Against Despotism

Such conflicting ideas about America surely may be found all through the interwar period, but they were going to be affected decisively by the changes in the world around 1930.

The economic depression which began in the United States in 1929 soon spread everywhere. The totalitarian powers began their victorious offensive. Japan pushed into China in 1931, Hitler took over the government of Germany in 1932. The military victories of the dictators in Ethiopia, the Rhineland, and Spain demonstrated the impotence of the League of Nations; purges revealed the internal weakness of the Soviet Union. The occupation of Austria and Czechoslovakia in 1938 and the Soviet-German pact in 1939 proved to be overtures to war.

Small Norway, without military might or defensive alliances, felt this mounting pressure strongly. Still, it was absorbed in its own economic situation. Beginning in 1930, the international crisis struck the country hard. By 1933 the plight of many farmers was desperate.

One-third of the organized labor force was out of work, and now there was no longer a refuge behind the ocean. But, parallel to developments in Denmark and Sweden, the result was not a further radicalization. The elections of 1930 demonstrated that a revolutionary line in the spirit of class struggle had no support among Norwegians. Before the next election, the Labor party adopted a broadly popular policy of peaceful reform within the framework of parliamentarism, climaxed by a realistic emergency program worked out together with the farmers under the slogan: "The Entire People To Work." Behind this basic change of ideology were the totalitarian threats abroad and at home: the new "popular front" was to defend democracy itself against the dangers from the extreme right. In 1935 the Labor party took over the government and remained at the helm for almost thirty years.

Contemporary developments in the United States here offered obvious parallels. Franklin D. Roosevelt came to power out of a similar economic debacle and tried to solve the crisis by similar planning within the existing system. The New Deal did not deeply influence the details of this development in Norway, but it threw fresh material into the discussion.

Many Norwegian Conservatives were bound to regard Roosevelt's policies with great skepticism. Most of the economists in principle did not believe in political interference with economic life. Roosevelt's measures allegedly were just a new American form of socialism: "through planned economy to dictatorship and starvation." In 1938 an anonymous Norwegian pamphlet was published with the title *Stop Roosevelt Now!* The President was accused of having killed America's purchasing power, "the dollar, that symbol of vigorous he-man-ship, as it was at the time of George Washington, Lincoln, McKinley and Theodore Roosevelt." The same repudiation sometimes was found on the extreme left. *Mot Dag* admitted that American capitalists were unprejudiced in their experimentation, but the production system remained unscathed. Roosevelt's reforms were "a capitalist remedy all through" and "a demonstration of all the impassable roads."

But there were also less narrow views. A number of non-socialist commentators in the 1930s discussed the New Deal from a psychological point of view. To these observers, the greatest contribution of Roosevelt was to unsettle the social notions of Americans, sowing doubts about competition and success. One of the leading Norwegian shipowners, Leif Höegh (1896-1974), through a period of five years published three articles on Roosevelt. He severely criticized his dabbling in planned economy, but at the same time he judged harshly that negative and passive capitalist policy which had made the New Deal necessary. Roosevelt's social reforms had been needed and largely successful. Above all, by his personality, Roosevelt had revived his nation's faith in the future, awakened the slumbering social conscience even in business, and strengthened the sense of immaterial values.

There were similar ideas on the radical side. Erling Falk had an old affection for democratic America as different from imperialist Great Britain, and tried to curb the anti-Americanism of his younger collaborators. He regarded Lincoln as the greatest statesman in history, beside Cromwell and ahead of Lenin. In Falk's journal *Mot Dag* in the 1930s there was little of that frenzied agitation against America that was customary in the Soviet Union, and the country was not singled out as a target in the fight against capitalism. Toward the end of the period, the younger writers of the group rather gave expression to a new optimism, partly as a result of Roosevelt's contribution: public opinion was changing fast in America and the workers were adding to their strength at an amazing rate. Soon they might be a match for the power of Wall Street.

The most lasting performance of the *Mot Dag* group was the publication of the six-volume *Workers' Encyclopedia* (1932-1936). Erling Falk himself wrote its warm biography of Lincoln. In its other articles there was the same cautious faith in America's radical future: workers and farmers now seemed to join forces in the United States as they had in revolutionary Russia. In 1939 a former group member publicly paid homage to Roosevelt as a symbol of a developing democracy and a society on the road to finding itself.

Decisive was, however, the development within the Labor party.

In economic policy, a Norwegian three-year plan was published in 1933. Many of its suggestions remained on paper. If depression subsided from the mid-1930s, it was due to general economic conditions more than to the plan, in Norway as in the United States. In both places, however, planning itself was felt as a mighty encouragement. The programs in many ways were similar, and in a general way there was a connection. The catastrophe in the United States engendered widespread doubts about the blessings of free enterprise. Even to many Liberals, the "passive state" now was felt to be out of date. But the particulars were rarely borrowed from the United States. American ventures were well known in Norway, but the ideas of J. M. Keynes and the experiences of Russia were more important to the Norwegian planners.

One general result of the New Deal, however, was the strengthening of a more optimistic view of the United States. This image now gradually was to become a real factor, even outside the field of economic policies, as part of changing attitudes within the Labor party.

The Norwegian Social Democrats did not only inaugurate a broad popular cooperation toward immediate practical aims. Under the increasing pressure of totalitarian movements in Norway and elsewhere, the Labor party also naturally came to emphasize more than before the value of traditional Norwegian democracy, in which even the workers now had a real share. Gradually, Socialists began using as their own the national symbols which hitherto had been regarded as bourgeois. Workers joined the general citizens' parades on Constitution Day, singing the national anthem under Norwegian (not red) banners. More and more frequently their speakers pointed back to Norwegian history: the labor movement was going to "finish the work begun at Eidsvoll in 1814" in the spirit of Henrik Wergeland.

This does not mean that the Socialist party looked to contemporary America as a model, but the role which America had played in the growth of Norwegian popular government was remembered and appreciated; in this, the historian Halvdan Koht was instrumental. He always had been of the opinion that Norwegian Socialists had continued the development started at Eidsvoll, and he believed that the same growth was now under way on both sides of the Atlantic. In 1937 a Socialist leader explicitly placed the labor movement in the context of the Declaration of Independence and its French and Norwegian successors. In the same year, in a speech on Constitution Day, another Labor leader compared the struggle in

1814 and present resistance against totalitarianism, summing up the goal in Lincoln's words: government "of the people, by the people, for the people."

Anxiety was bound to increase steadily toward the end of the 1930s. As the economic pressure lightened at home, the dividing lines in foreign policy stood out with great clarity. The Moscow trials killed all sympathy for the Soviet Union and reduced the Norwegian Communist party to insignificance. The Fascist and Nazi sympathizers had no great following either; Quisling's comparisons between the "democracies of Stalin and Wall Street" found little response. But behind them loomed the military might of the new Germany, and important Conservative papers in Norway now tried to look "objectively" at the totalitarian systems, black and brown. When in 1936 the Nobel prize was granted to the imprisoned German pacifist Carl von Ossietzky, Knut Hamsun protested publicly.

Because of this double pressure, it was inevitable that the position and future role of the United States should increasingly come to the fore in Norwegian thought and that the United States should become the focus of hope. The great problem, of course, was isolationism, which still formally governed American foreign policy. But more and more it was now maintained that this attitude could not possibly last long in the present world situation. Norwegian observers in the United States reported widespread concern there for the future of democracy in the world; they found a genuine indignation toward the dictatorships and a growing realization that the country could not avoid becoming involved in "the great settlement." The United States was pointed to as the potential "rescuer of the world."

A distinctive part in this regard was played by the Conservative leader C. J. Hambro. His view of America changed radically during the 1930s, perhaps under the influence of the Oxford Movement. Instead of his previous admiration of the United States as the financial giant, there was now a growing distrust of that complacent business optimism and that uncontrolled private initiative which he had before eulogized. He displayed skepticism toward Henry Ford and concern about both the lack of real liberty and the air of "cruelty and hard-heartedness" in the United States; he even feared a possible American Fascism supported by capital. He saw Roosevelt as the only alternative to all the totalitarian movements and as the potential leader in a "universal policy of ideas" to save the democratic world.

The clearest spokesman of this thought was Halvdan Koht, from 1935 minister of foreign affairs in the Labor government. He last had visited the United States in 1930 and had been shocked by the "almost inconceivable destitution" and political decay there. But he was even more surprised by the general feeling among Americans that capitalism itself was bankrupt: "Nobody can stop the American advance toward socialism." The contribution of Franklin D. Roosevelt formed a part of this picture: he had "made social responsibility a living element in American politics, even within the system of private capitalism."

In the 1930s this development confirmed Koht's conviction that Europe could still count on the United States. In his own policy, he emphasized that the two countries now saw eye-to-eye on the great questions. As the first Norwegian minister of foreign affairs, he visited America officially in 1937. In his speech upon arrival, he reminded his listeners that Norway and the United States stood for the same political ideals and that the small nations put their trust in America in the work for "peace, justice and mutual respect." At the same time, in interviews upon his return to Norway, he rejoiced in the keen social interest he had found in America, attributing it to the New Deal, and praised the development of a national labor movement in sympathy with similar movements in Norway.

In Koht's futile effort since the late 1930s to use the League of Nations as an instrument to prevent the war, he had enjoyed at least a general support in the appeals of President Roosevelt for peace and disarmament. In 1939 a feeling of fellowship was expressed officially when the Norwegian government sent the crown prince and crown princess of Norway on a successful friendship tour of the United States. Koht, as acting prime minister, interpreted this gesture as a sign that the Norwegians too believed in freedom and democracy and intended to keep and support these ideals.

The feeling of fellowship was also expressed in articles published just before the outbreak of World War II by Justice of the Norwegian Supreme Court Ferdinand Schjelderup (1886-1955), who became one of the leaders of the Norwegian resistance movement during the German occupation. In 1938 the editors of the Norwegian *Journal of Jurisprudence* stated that, in a period when the reign of law was being repudiated in one country after another, even that journal might be called upon to defend actively the idea of justice. In the same volume, there were three articles on American subjects. The article by Ferdinand Schjelderup discussed the growth of democracy in America under the Constitution. In spring 1940 Schjelderup wrote in the same journal an article entitled "The Principle of Justice in American Constitutional Law." He referred to the ideas of Eidsvoll and maintained that they had to be upheld "if the soil of Norway is going to remain free." At the time of publication, Norway had already been occupied by Nazi Germany.

§

CHAPTER 8

Scared New World 1940-

World history during and after World War II in many ways represented a continuation of the history of previous decades. However, the period was marked by perhaps the most momentous upheavals known in history, changes both in the world itself and in its relation to the United States. To many present-day readers, these events have the closeness of experience and are thus deprived of perspective. They are loaded with emotions and therefore sober judgment is difficult. Often they have no previous parallels; evaluation then becomes tentative. Even in little Norway the amount of material is massive. This chapter can only select a few points that are of obvious importance.

The War, 1940-1945

Norway hoped to stay neutral in World War II, as did the United

States. The successful German lightning attack in April 1940 put Norway at a disadvantage, but the two months' war on Norway's own soil demonstrated its willingness to fight, and during the operation the German navy suffered losses which never were fully repaired. The Norwegian government established in exile in London was not only constitutionally legal but had at its disposal great resources, above all 1,000 modern and high-speed merchant ships of 4 million brutto tons, manned by crews which totaled 30,000 men.

From the outbreak of the war, President Franklin D. Roosevelt indefatigably tried to assist the Allies in spite of the American neutrality laws. The Norwegian merchant marine was an indispensable link in the transport of war material across the Atlantic. Norway also participated actively in the convoy service; among other things, it utilized some of the ships made available by Roosevelt's famous "destroyer deal." The Norwegian government in 1941 signed the Atlantic Charter, and Roosevelt emphasized Norway's role as a respected ally in many ways. Exiled Norwegian royalty were well received in America. The Norwegian government signed its own Lend-Lease agreement with the United States, and the military forces of both countries worked closely together.

For a small nation like Norway, wartime cooperation with the great Allies naturally was not without friction; this was even more the case when the Soviet Union, Norway's neighbor, entered the war. Thus, in 1942 Churchill and Roosevelt agreed on the preparations for an Allied winter attack on occupied Norway. The Norwegians themselves were far from enthusiastic, and the plans were shelved, together with other suggestions of the same kind. In 1943 Roosevelt, apparently on his own initiative, hinted at the possibility of offering the Soviet Union a couple of free ports in northern Norway, an old idea which was bluntly rejected by the Norwegian government and never was heard of again.

Such differences of opinion remained secret, however, and did not affect the Norwegians' feeling of confidence toward their mighty ally. Correspondingly, Norway played its part in building morale within the United States itself. Misleading initial reports about the Norwegian attitude toward the invaders were soon refuted. American public opinion was impressed by the fact that in 1942 Norwegian ships carried across the Atlantic 50 percent of all fuel and 30 percent of all other supplies for the Allies; military leaders called the Norwegian merchant marine "much more valuable than an army of one million men." Americans noted with satisfaction that the Norwegian exiled government was able to pay its expenses, including interest on Norwegian prewar loans. Above all, Americans were impressed by reports about the Norwegian resistance movement, particularly the activity of teachers and clergy.

As of old, "Norwegian America" was solidly isolationist. Norway's fight largely changed the picture, as witnessed by the huge amounts of money collected by Norwegian-Americans for the reconstruction of the country after the war. Roosevelt probably gave expression to widespread sentiments when, in a speech in 1942, he made Norway a symbol of the democratic fighting spirit: "If there is anyone who still wonders why this war is being fought, let him look to Norway."

In the occupied country, Nazi propaganda initially was focused on Great Britain, but from 1942 onward the United States also came in for its full share. Vidkun Quisling described the American war effort as an instrument of international Jewry. The Allied, American, and Norwegian information which reached the country both from Great Britain and the United States had much greater effect. The human warmth of Franklin D. Roosevelt's radio appeals moved the Norwegians, and his sudden death made a deep impression. America also played a part in Norwegian counter-propaganda in the country itself, as far as it was possible. In the university, lectures on American law and American history during the war surely displayed the art of "saying it without saying it."

At the same time, there was in occupied Norway a strong sympathy for the Soviet Union. The importance of the Russian military contribution was fully realized. Toward the end of the war, the Norwegian merchant marine suffered some of its heaviest losses in the transport of American supplies to Murmansk. Many Norwegians shared Roosevelt's hopes of a peaceful cooperation with the Soviet Union after the war. Russian soldiers finally expelled the Germans from northern Norway in cooperation with the Norwegians and properly withdrew when the fighting was over.

Toward the end of the war, American atomic bombs were dropped over Nagasaki and Hiroshima. This mass extinction of civilians was felt as a shock even in Norway, but it coincided with the ecstasy of liberation. Nobody at the time could fully realize the implications of the event.

Thus, the image of America in Norway, during the ensuing marvelous summer of peace and liberty, probably was more overwhelmingly positive than at any other point in the interrelationship of the two nations. In the fall of 1945 a book appeared, entitled *The Heritage of Eidsvoll,* in which well-known Norwegians tried to sum up the aims and stakes of the past war. Among the authors was the leader of the Home Front during the occupation, Chief Justice Paal Berg (1873-1968). In his article, he demonstrated that the United States, during the war years 1940-1945, had been the great champion of Norwegian traditions. He surely gave expression to the ideas and feelings of the large majority of his fellow-countrymen.

The New World

That new world where, in the future, Norway and the United States were to live together very soon proved to differ widely from all expectations, however, and to have dimensions which gave a new sense even to old ideas. Development ran at an increasing pace all through the period, and clear distinctions cannot be drawn. But the results were conspicuous and, in many ways, new. A British historian has distinguished the thirty years from 1945 to 1975 as fundamentally different, naming the period the "post-modern time."

The main factor was the breakthrough of technology on a global scale. The roots went far back, but after 1945 expansion became explosive, comprising the most important parts of the world and the essential areas of human existence. Everywhere, development took the same forms of industrialization, commercialization, urbanization and suburbanization, automation, standardization, and centralization, all made possible by the data machine. And everywhere, the development pointed toward a uniform consumers' society based on physical comfort.

Technique wiped out what was left of geographical distance. It equally eliminated intellectual distance by telecommunication systems which overcame language barriers. In the industrialized societies of the present day, everybody is able to see and hear from hour to hour everything on earth that the program makers find it worthwhile to see and hear.

This is just one aspect of the general interrelation and interentanglement of the new world. The political vibrations are felt through the entire cobweb. National border lines are increasingly meaningless, as demonstrated drastically during the oil crises. The new forms of production are largely the same everywhere. In the wider area of civilization, new transnational groups originate, molded by mass-produced magazines and pocketbooks, movies and radio, TV and recorded sound, often on a world basis. It is a change that makes the nineteenth-century industrial revolution appear as halfway and modest and makes even the interwar period seem provincial. Through atomic power and the use of outer space, the transformation takes on aspects that sometimes point beyond what is human, in the traditional sense of the word.

In the 1970s this new form of life is still in the beginning stages, but even as early as 1945 its direction was obvious. And it also became evident early that in many fields this development was bound to raise new problems and create new relations between powers.

Politically and militarily, the world in 1945 might appear as relatively simple. It was dominated by two pyramidal superpowers, the capitalist United States and the Communist Soviet Union; in the words of Henrik Wergeland, their shadows met in powerless Germany. In this game the United States seemed to hold all the cards: it had unscathed resources, a monopoly on atomic weapons, and it was the summit of a capitalistic system which, through its European influence, comprised the larger part of the world.

But this situation changed completely in the course of a few years. With unbelievable rapidity, the colonies of the European powers threw off their shackles. The universal ideology of communism held out the promise of an industrial revolution for the benefit of all and appealed to the masses far more effectively than did capitalism. Soon, Marxism in various forms gathered behind it about one-third of the earth's population, including giant-sized China. Other new states, numerous and populous, preferred to remain neutral in the battle of ideologies. At the same time, Western Europe and Japan gained strength again as huge industrial powers. Atomic weapons came into ever more hands. The United States was confronted with new constellations and combinations and had a smaller technical and industrial lead than before.

Nevertheless, America still held immense power, both economically and militarily. Capital increased its concentration within America itself and gained a mighty effectiveness abroad through multinational concerns. These organizations are highly controversial and, because of secrecy, their actual power is hard to grasp. But they are real, probably the most typical expression of the globalization of the world. Their combined power is enormous, and the most important and strongest of them have their center in the United States.

Figures here have to be approximate, but if today a total of $270 billion of nongovernment money is invested in the international financial market, probably around $110 billion will be in the hands of companies subsidiary to American-based multinational concerns. Other estimates make the American part even larger. According to the nature of these organizations, they try to turn the entire world within their reach into one homogeneous supermarket. By their invasion of capital, they are spreading American (often that just means modern) methods of production and marketing, forms of business management, ways of thinking, and general ideologies all over the world.

This gigantic system is not directed by its directors. It has a willpower of its own, a built-in acceleration which is in the system itself, regardless of nationality. Even outside the United States, coordination is now the slogan in the fight for power, in Europe as in the oil states. Everywhere, production demands a higher standard of living, an increased purchasing power, new expansion, new resources, and new markets. Stagnation more and more spells catastrophe.

This growth poses world problems of a new magnitude. For the first time in history, responsible experts are earnestly asking how long a development of this kind can continue in view of the earth's limited natural resources. Even more urgent is the problem of how, under the new stresses and pressures, it will be possible to maintain on earth such living conditions that human beings may thrive or, quite simply, survive, particularly in the underdeveloped countries.

In many ways, this new world must appear as terrifying, like an ominous game of anonymous economic forces. These forces are intangible, without face and human responsibility, but nobody can doubt the enormous power in their hands. They have some of their most important bases in the United States. And something similar also holds true in the area of culture.

Nobody could today imagine using the adjective "American" about the international consumers' civilization which is now springing up everywhere around the globe. Similar forces are creating similar results wherever they are working. This is especially the case today on both sides of the Atlantic. Within the new "Euromerica" which is taking shape, old frictions and shades of difference now often appear as negligible or even ludicrous. Communication and cultural exchange of goods are so intensive and mutual influence so continuous that similarity often must appear as more dominant than difference. The rest of the world feels the unity most definitely.

But part of this Western civilization doubtless is of American origin, has an American trademark, and shows certain features characteristic of America. They do not always represent the essential values of the American tradition. Rather, the picture is dominated by cheapness and saleability, the emptiness of technique and the synthetic optimism of advertising. Those are the features that are often distributed most widely and reach the biggest audience, supported by American capital with its automatic and impersonal mass effect. These are the aspects which now are provoking counter-movements most strongly, partly in the old national states of Europe, but even more in the large world of developing nations.

This is not just a reaction born of nationalism. Often, the resistance springs from doubts based on a philosophy of life and from a deep anxiety about the new form of existence. Hesitations of this kind about America have been uttered many times in the past. Now they often are built on a more thorough understanding of the general powers, economic and social, which create this kind of civilization and which, so far, have been brought under human control but imperfectly.

Happy Harmony

When Norway began putting its house in order after the great ordeal, few could suspect, let alone foresee, such developments. There were more pleasant things to think of.

The liberation days in the spring and summer of 1945 were the largest popular celebration in Norwegian history. In addition to homage to their own national heroes, there was also a deep-felt gratitude among Norwegians toward their comrades-in-arms outside Norway who had made liberation possible. The English and the Russians were the first objects of Norway's gratitude, but a wave of warm feelings also went to the United States, and the arrival of so many good gifts from "Norwegian America" gave the sympathy a touch of the personal and palpable. This positive sentiment had its focus in the late President Roosevelt. His statue in front of the Oslo City Hall was dedicated by Eleanor Roosevelt in 1950; he was the only foreign statesman besides Abraham Lincoln to be thus honored in the Norwegian capital. As late as 1952 Dwight Eisenhower was warmly received in Oslo as a great war hero.

Internal problems were, of course, Norway's first preoccupation at this time. In the international field, tensions had not yet reappeared. There was great confidence in the United Nations, which was the creation jointly of Woodrow Wilson and Franklin D. Roosevelt and had its headquarters in the United States. The Nobel Peace prizes granted successively to Roosevelt's Secretary of State Cordell Hull (1945), Emily G. Balch and John R. Mott (1946), and the UN leader Ralph Bunche (1950) were a sign of this faith in American constructive pacifism.

The foreign policy of Norway itself immediately after the war fitted into this picture: the country would serve as a bridge builder between the two superpowers without any direct alignment. Norway happily accepted the Marshall Plan for international economic recovery, and on its part received a direct American subsidy of about 2.7 billion Norwegian crowns.

But at the same time there were also more skeptical voices, reminding of other realities. The war dealt a deathblow to the traditional Norwegian faith in neutrality. During the first years of the war, the government in exile in London seriously discussed, and rejected, the idea of an Atlantic military alliance after the war. But developments soon brought such ideas to the fore again. "Peaceful coexistence" proved to mean different things East and West. In 1946 Churchill for the first time pointed to the "iron curtain" going down in Europe, as the Soviet Union enforced its political system in one neighboring country after another. When, in 1947, the turn came for Turkey and Greece, the Truman Doctrine made it clear to the world that the United States, and nobody else, now was determined and had the power to draw a demarcation line limiting Communist expansion. At the same time, Soviet diplomatic pressure on the Norwegian government with regard to the future status of Spitzbergen (Svalbard) was felt as a warning that even the northern neighbors of the Russians might soon be in need of protection.

Decisive to Norwegian opinion was the Soviet intervention in Czechoslovakia in 1948, together with the death of Jan Masaryk. He and his nation had been regarded as the main champions of the peaceful bridge building between the East and the West. To the Norwegians, the events in Praha came as a terrifying shock. At the same time, the Soviet Union demanded from the Finns a military treaty of friendship. The Norwegian government had reason to expect that a similar demand would soon be directed at Norway and decided to refuse. In this situation, the United States appeared as the only possible guarantor of future Norwegian liberty of action. The blockade of Berlin and the American air bridge in the summer of 1948 gave strength to the same idea.

The Western great powers were already discussing a military alliance. The Norwegian government decided to participate in these negotiations, and in 1949 Norway joined NATO (the North Atlantic Treaty Organization) together with the Nordic states of Denmark and Iceland. Important to the decision of the Labor government was a strong plea for participation from Halvdan Koht. The pact was sensational. For the first time in its history, pacifist and social democratic Norway entered a formal military alliance. Its partner was the dominant capitalist power. The treaty was signed in order to make possible a rearmament on a large scale, openly directed against Communist power in the East.

Resistance to this alliance was inevitable, but the fight against NATO found scant support in the beginning. Memories of the war and confidence in the United States were still alive. The ruling Labor party harbored an ingrained suspicion toward Moscow, and a majority of the population just felt the alliance to be necessary. Such ideas were vindicated by the continued manifestations of Communist power politics, headlined by Korea in 1950, Berlin in 1953, Hungary in 1956, the Berlin wall in 1961, and, above all, the second rape of Czechoslovakia in 1968. The impression of these events in Norway was increasingly violent. To the great majority of the population, they confirmed the conviction that NATO might well have prevented Norway from being in a similar position. When President John F. Kennedy in Berlin in 1963 called himself "ein Berliner," it was felt as an American guarantee even to the smaller allies. If Kennedy's violent death made a deep impression on Norway, the shock had a background in such considerations.

Regardless of great politics, the organization of NATO itself made rapid progress with its North European headquarters in Oslo and its infrastructure of communication systems, airports, military installations, and stores. To a considerable extent, the equipment was paid for or delivered free of charge by Norway's allies, above all by the United States, at a total cost of between 4 and 5 billion Norwegian crowns.

Norwegian daily life was not influenced by the alliance, however. An American uniform is hardly ever to be seen in Oslo. Nor has the free expression of opinion been hampered in the slightest. But until the 1960s there was no need of harsh criticism. The effective distribution of news after the war made all aspects of contemporary America well known in Norway. But an efficient American information service gave balance to the picture and strengthened the feeling of sympathy.

In 1949 the Norwegian minister of foreign affairs soberly stated the reasons why Norway had entered NATO: Norway would gain peace and security "by cooperation with states which have the same kind of political institutions, have a similar understanding of democracy, and are living under approximately comparable economic conditions." In Norwegian opinion, the America of Franklin D. Roosevelt did not deviate too much from that image.

As early as 1945 one of the most magnificent social projects of Roosevelt's presidential period was recalled to the memory of Norwegian readers in Georg Brochmann's book on the Tennessee Valley Authority, subtitled *Democracy and Planning.* Many aspects of American internal policy in the postwar years showed these traditions not to be defunct. Several of Roosevelt's successors in the presidency declared themselves to be his spiritual heirs and in their work tried to continue along the same line. Norwegian readers were able to follow this development in considerable detail, both in newspapers and books, from Truman's Fair Deal and Kennedy's New Frontier to Lyndon B. Johnson's Great Society. Kennedy's personal "new style" certainly made a positive impression. Important were the efforts of racial integration, climaxed by the Supreme Court decision on desegregation in the schools, made in 1954 on the Norwegian Constitution Day. The Nobel Peace prize granted to Martin Luther King in 1964 also implied a recognition of American racial policies.

Ideology was not all-important during these early years, however. Once the NATO shield was in its place, it was no longer in the public eye. To the average Norwegian, day-to-day politics in the United States was of no great concern. What was close and visible to everybody was the immediate postwar American influence on Norwegian economic and daily life. Here, too, the interplay now had dimensions unparalleled before.

To a considerable extent, this growth was due to an influx of American capital. In the 1950s foreign investments in Norway were still below the prewar level. But they were increasing, and the Americans now were on top. By 1968 foreign investments in Norwegian industry and commerce amounted to around one-fifth of the total, and almost 30 percent of that was American; the second nation on the list, Great Britain, stood for about 15 percent. These figures apply to direct investments only; the American portion would be much greater if the account included investments through subsidiaries of American-based multinational concerns and other forms of indirect foreign control. In addition, Norway received huge financial assistance under the Marshall Plan and the NATO program. This supply of American money was an important factor in the rapid economic expansion in Norway through which, by the late 1960s, the national product in absolute figures had multiplied more than five times compared to the prewar period, and the country had reached a living standard among the highest in Europe.

The influx of capital was just one side of the picture. Perhaps equally important was the impact of American industrial know-how and business management. The contacts established in the interwar period now were much extended by organized cooperation under the Marshall Plan. All over Western Europe in the 1950s "study groups" and "productivity committees" left for the United States and returned with fresh knowledge. In Norway, too, a great number of study reports from such expeditions was published, covering many fields, from agriculture and industrial organization to computer technique and public relations. Even more extensive were individual contacts. Of the numerous travel grants made available after the war, a great many were used for the study of American business management.

Tracing the influence of this experience would be futile; it was only a part of the swiftly increasing general interplay. A yardstick may be the direct physical connection between the countries. In spite of the gradual shift of passenger and freight traffic to the airlines, the number of Norwegian ships in American harbors doubled between 1938 and 1965. The exchange of goods shows the same picture. Norwegian exports to the United States in 1939 amounted to a value of 84 million Norwegian crowns, in 1973 to 1,443 million. Imports in the same years showed figures of 147 million and 2,215 million, at the current rate of exchange.

Such figures mean that in Norway, as everywhere in Western Europe, American products of all kinds are today for sale in astonishing plenty. Whoever enters a Norwegian shopping center (closely modeled on its American namesake) will find on the shelves numerous goods of American make, from juice to cereals. Others are made in Norway or Europe on American license or just copy the American brands, and they all look alike. The same picture prevails in toy shops with their countless plastic imitations, in clothing shops which sell cowboy pants and Davy Crockett hats, and in all kinds of specialized stores for kitchen equipment and tools, office machines and cosmetics. Here, variation and change are endless and continuous, dependent on many factors. For instance, American-built cars by now are rare on Norwegian roads. But more often than not the two transatlantic markets are insensibly fused.

Even more conspicuous than the products themselves is the marketing that goes with them. Here national differences are now blurring fast. There is a direct line from the advertising sections in American magazines and their dreamworld of glossy high life to the somewhat less sophisticated Norwegian imitations. To sell in Norway, goods need English names. The coarsest baits are just taken over, from the "keep-young" appeal to Mother's Day. The American style of life imperceptibly slips in together with its appurtenances, usually with the original names intact, from snack bars and soft ice to rock and twist. Nobody considers anymore whether all of this is "Norwegian" or "American."

On the same current comes the mass-produced word. A somewhat good-sized Norwegian newsstand today presents the same selection of American printed matter as do the majority of such stands everywhere else in Europe, from _Time_ and _Newsweek_ and the overseas editions of American newspapers to all the more obscure publications and the piles of pocketbooks. (The number of Norwegians who know English is a surprise to foreign visitors.) The _Readers' Digest_ in its Norwegian edition has had a large circulation ever since the war. Norwegian imitations often come close to their American models. American material in the ordinary Norwegian weeklies is immense.

Donald Duck represents a special case. In Sweden and Denmark, he was introduced under national names; in Norway he is accepted as he is. There are countless native comics which imitate American originals. Their circulation runs into the hundred thousands, and their impact is palpable. Norwegian fishing boats are no longer named for Leiv Eiriksson, George Washington, and Benjamin Franklin, but are called Polly, Daisy, and Blondy.

The entertainment industry deserves a separate dissertation. The mass media are now gradually being molded into one great international show business. There is still much variation, with leeway both for individual nations and for personally distinctive artists, but "American" characteristics are still holding their own and often are predominant. In the movies, in 1951 American films made up 63 percent of all imports, and in the early 1970s the figure still was between 40 and 50 percent. The mythical figures of the American dreamworld are as vivid in the popular imagination in Norway as were once the heroes of the fairy tales. Even productions from other countries often look or sound "American" regardless of origin, on the screen, the telescreen, or the stage.

The same internationalization is typical in music. In a statistical breakdown of foreign music played in movies, radio, television, and on the stage in Norway in 1973, America topped the list. High-quality products in the field are now common in Norway as every-where, from the classics to the blues. The names of American musicians and singers are household words, from Ella and Louis to Bernstein and Joan Baez. Irving Berlin and Elvis Presley are every-day realities to thousands of Norwegians who have no knowledge of the "great" names of music, national or foreign.

American pop, of course, holds the central place, resounds from all juke boxes, has the mass sale in records, tape, and cassettes, and dominates at the many "festivals." When farm youths at the River Laagen in central Norway formed a band, they named it *The Deep Laagen Boys.* Both the ballads and Edvard Grieg are now being ar-ranged in jazz style, to the delight of connoisseurs. The American gospel-singing style has penetrated into the religious field as well.

In addition, a significant number of Norwegians have gained personal knowledge of America. Even in the interwar period, rela-tively few Norwegians visited the United States, emigrants apart. After 1945 the living standard soared in most of the Western coun-tries, and so did traveling. Going abroad suddenly became com-mon even for average Norwegians, who traveled particularly in the Old World, but gradually in the New as well. Norwegians crossed the Atlantic by charter flights of various kinds. Youngsters did the same on fellowships, in particular under the American Field Service, and often, before they returned, they had traveled cheaply across half of the continent by Greyhound bus. The intimacy of personal experience, which in earlier generations was reserved for emigrants, now was enjoyed by large numbers of Norwegians.

Within this exchange, even what could once be called "Norwegian America" now took its natural place, without illusions on either side. Cultural contacts have been kept alive as far as possible across the language barrier. Historical memories have been cherished at a respectful distance. Norwegian-Americans fly "home" on "family tours" with mixed feelings of alienation and nostalgic attachment.

When in 1975, at the 150th anniversary of emigration, the King and the Prime Minister of Norway separately toured the major Norwegian settlements in the United States, it was an appropriate act of homage, moving almost exclusively in the realm of emotions.

The widened contact shows most when it comes to literary translation. Its rapid growth in the interwar years continued, parallel to the explosive expansion of book production as a whole. In the five-year period from 1946 to 1950, a little more than 700 titles of English-language belles lettres were translated into Norwegian, and in the period from 1965 to 1970 almost 2,200. Up to 1970 more than half of the titles were American; after 1970 the British and Commonwealth titles together were in the majority, although in some subject areas, American books still prevailed. Thus, in 1973, eighty-seven American children's books were translated, and only twenty-two British.

No breakdown can be given here of the percentage, among all these translations, of sex and crime books and junk of other kinds, published on speculation. Surely it is high. At the same time, however, serious contemporary creative writing was well represented on the publication lists; some of it even showed high sales figures. Hemingway still held the lead; in 1961 the second largest public library of Norway reported him to be "the most popular writer of all," Norwegian writers included. By 1962 he had appeared in twenty-four Norwegian editions, and the total sales figure for his novels was 270,000 copies, almost the same as in Sweden, whose population is twice as big. In 1973 one could see, in Norwegian newspapers large and small, a full-page portrait of Hemingway to advertise his books. His collected works have been published in Norwegian; there is no such edition in English.

Even more interesting is the evident intention, after 1945, among both Norwegian publishers and translators, to give a decent picture of all of the valuable literature of America, not only of the bestsellers. Several collections of first-rate American short stories and two general anthologies of American poetry appeared in Norwegian translation, several of them covering American literature from the eighteenth century onward. Among the classics of the nineteenth century there were, after the war, one translation of Thoreau's _Walden_ and two of Hawthorne's _The Scarlet Letter,_ one volume of Poe's poems and critical prose, versions of Longfellow's *Hiawatha* and Whitman's *Song of Myself,* and four novels by Herman Melville. With respect to later American writers, some of the worst gaps were filled by translations from Henry James, Stephen Crane, Theodore Dreiser, and Edgar Lee Masters.

Most striking is the interest in the poetry of the interwar years and the years after World War II. The list includes collections by T. S. Eliot, Ezra Pound, and William Carlos Williams, anthologies of lyrical poems and pop songs since 1945, and separate volumes by Robert Bly, Robert Creeley, and Allen Ginsberg. The repertories of the theaters probably would show a similar picture. For a nation of 4 million, this is a respectable performance. How deeply American writing has influenced Norwegian authors in their own work only the future can tell. But the impact often is striking both in the traditional genres and in the new and "formless" types, the songs of protest, and the modern ballads, which have suddenly gained a tremendous popularity.

One special field can only be touched upon: the translations of popular American books of information for everyday life. As an example, popular volumes on child care should be mentioned. The main work of the most widely circulated American writer in the field, Dr. Benjamin Spock, up to 1974 had sold 65,000 copies in a country where such books normally have a printing of 2,000-5,000. American children's books are here supplemented on a more scholarly level.

A special but noticeable side effect of this interplay is the British-American influence on language. As of old, German loan words were common in Norwegian; after World War II Anglo-Saxon words penetrated with equal force. Norwegians home from British or American war service often brought back technical terms. Even more all-pervading was the effect of movies, television, literature, and advertising. Being in a permanent state of flux, the Norwegian idiom itself had little power of resistance. Particularly among the younger generation, the phenomenon directly reflects the impact of an American way of life.

This sequence of events has been more or less automatic: American elements slipped into the cultural pattern insensibly, to an extent unmatched before. Simultaneously, the postwar period is characterized by its determined and planned effort toward a conscious evaluation of America and Americans, and by the large amount of material made available in the service of such judgments.

The wide reading of American printed matter and the quantity of Americana in movies, radio, and television in Norway present much food for thought. The first serious effort to supplement this material systematically was made by the Americans themselves through the United States information offices and libraries which were opened in Norway as soon as hostilities came to an end and ever since have offered a current news and book service. From 1946 there was also an Associated Press bureau in Oslo. Most important, since the war the Norwegian news media have covered America and its problems on a level and with a professional competence unheard-of before. The average Norwegian now has access to regular American reports and commentaries on radio and television, most often by experts on the spot, making the United States a part of his day-to-day and hour-to-hour picture of the world.

For those who read books, even popular informational literature about America is now both more extensive and better. There are solid American histories by James Truslow Adams (1945) and Ingrid Semmingsen (1946, 1972), and the United States has been given broad coverage in general works on world history and world literature. In the postwar period, between thirty and forty biographies of Americans, translated or original, have appeared in Norway; among their subjects were Columbus (one book), Franklin (three), Jefferson (one), Lincoln (four), the Roosevelt family (eight), Eisenhower (two), and J. F. Kennedy (three). There is also a book about all of the American presidents. John D. Rockefeller, J. P. Morgan, and Henry Ford were represented by only one biography each. Books have appeared about Americans as different as Thorstein Veblen, Ralph Nader, Jack London, John R. Mott, Paul Robeson, Joe Louis, Helen Keller, and Walt Disney. There are works by contemporary American politicians and political commentators, a number of travel accounts, serious books of debate, and a worthwhile literature of essays.

Even in scholarship the interrelation now takes on new forms.

Most striking is the exchange of persons, within all possible fields. Since 1947 the American (from 1958: International) Summer School of the University of Oslo every year has taken several hundred foreign students to Norway for six weeks' study of the country. Regardless of the name of the school, the majority of the students have been American. Among foreign students (Scandinavian countries not included), Americans usually have formed the largest group. A long series of fellowships, Norwegian and American, has made it possible for a great number of Norwegian youngsters to spend time at American institutions of education. Evaluation and recognition of American examinations now are routine at Norwegian universities.

On a higher level, the Fulbright, Smidt, Mundt, and Hays arrangements, with their generous fellowships, have offered hundreds of American scholars the opportunity to do research work and, quite often, also to teach at Norwegian universities. The same arrangements and similar American and Norwegian fellowships, particularly under the Rockefeller Foundation and the American Council of Learned Societies, have made Norwegian studies and research in America equally common.

The scholarly results of these efforts cannot be evaluated here, but in some fields the influence is striking. At Norwegian universities there are subjects today in which the bulk of recommended literature is American. Of particular interest is the impact from disciplines in which America once played an insignificant part. As examples in the humanities may be mentioned the influence of the New Criticism on literary studies, of American philosophy and sociology, and even of American theology.

At the center of this contact is the systematic study of American civilization, in which secondary schools made the beginning. Soon after the war they successfully demanded that American literature and "background" (history of civilization) be given space in curricula and textbooks beside the traditional British material and that American pronunciation be recognized as well. A long series of summer courses with American support prepared teachers in such subjects, which had so far been neglected in their studies.

In 1946 the Norwegian government established at the University of Oslo a professorship of American literature; at the time, such chairs were extremely rare in Europe. With American and Norwegian financial support, large collections of books and material were gathered at the American Institute in Oslo. After some resistance, by the late 1950s American subjects were given the same status on the university level that they had already obtained in the secondary schools.

At the same time, the general number of students increased explosively. New universities had to be established, all of them with similar curricula. Suddenly, American studies was a big subject. For more than a decade, American Fulbright scholars had participated in regular teaching. Now the staff had to be added to on a more permanent basis, partly again with American financial support. A chair of American history was established in Oslo in 1963, and other chairs followed everywhere in rapid succession. At the three universities in southern Norway, there is today a total of three full professorships, two associate professorships, and six and a half lectureships of American literature and/or civilization, in addition to part-time scholarly staff. At the new university of Tromsö, the two professors of English literature and civilization are expected to cover both the American and the British fields. In proportion to the size of the population, there probably is a larger staff teaching American studies in Norway than in any other European country.

These studies also have offered a foundation for considerable scholarly research, developed under the influence of what the Americans themselves call "American studies," although the methods have been applied with a good deal of independence. The series of publications of the American Institute in Oslo by 1976 numbered fifteen sizable volumes. In addition, there were weighty Norwegian contributions in American history, jurisprudence, folklore, and education, and much research on emigration. Work in the history of American language, literature, and intellectual life has been especially strong. A central position has been held by the study of all kinds of transatlantic interrelations. Some of the main contributions in that field are mentioned in the preface of this book.

The most important of these comparative studies still bore witness to the confident attitude of the early postwar years. In particular this held true of Halvdan Koht's *American Spirit in Europe* (1949), which opened the series of publications of the American Institute. His book painted no roseate picture of the United States, but he was convinced that under President Roosevelt America had again become a nation on which other nations could rely in the fight for freedom.

Koht well saw the split between East and West in the postwar world, but to him the entire history of mankind pointed toward a gradual settlement between individualism and collectivism such as was now being attempted both in Norway and in other countries of Western Europe. Here he put his faith in America: he still saw it as "a young nation." In so many ways it had become "the very center of Western civilization," and it possessed that strength and belief in the future which was needed to build "the brave new world."

Janus or Medusa?

The first ten to fifteen years following the conclusion of hostilities in 1945 perhaps were the richest, and in many ways the happiest, period in the relationship between Norway and the United States. Never before had contacts been so many-sided and intense and the two countries felt themselves so closely united in a fellowship of real relevance.

But this union rested on clear suppositions. All through the historic relationship between Norway and America runs a continuous tension. In the 1960s, it reappeared. The Norwegian membership in NATO was based on the hope that the United States that had showed itself to the world in the great war had been the "real" America, a natural ally of Norway in ideas and attitudes toward life, not only an incidental partner in the cold game of power politics. What raised its head and gradually grew in force through the postwar years was a doubt that this judgment was correct.

During the great conflagration itself, a sober evaluation and a certain hesitation toward the United States was not unknown among Norwegians who knew the country, and not least among those who spent the war years in America. A similar critical balance of pros and cons could be found in Norwegian commentaries written soon after the peace: admiration for Franklin D. Roosevelt went together with anxieties created by "the new industrial revolution" with its "permanent crisis," its urge for expansion, and its probable aversion to social change in the countries of potential markets. Public discussion regarding NATO in 1948 and 1949 often had a strand of anti-Americanism. Demonstrations took place in Oslo when, in 1953, General Marshall received the Nobel Peace prize. Gradually, the objectors were given more to build on.

Initially, criticism was focused on internal circumstances in the United States. There was no illusion among initiated Norwegian observers about the ludicrous democracy in some of the so-called "democratic" states of Europe, but more was expected from the United States. The hardening of the social climate after the war was early noticed. But the first and general shock came with the McCarthy wave in the years from 1950 to 1954, when elementary democratic rights were disregarded in America under an anti-Communist mass hysteria which at times had the support of 50 percent of the population, according to Gallup polls. From the mid-1950s racial unrest took new and terrifying forms with increasing disturbance and use of arms, down to the Indian riots after 1970. The problem of American poverty was brought home even to Norwegians by the discussion around Michael Harrington's _The Other America_ (1962). The public atmosphere in the United States changed strikingly, with open confrontation and an increasing use of violence, climaxed by the political assassinations of the Kennedy brothers and Martin Luther King (1963, 1968).

The hippie movement and, even more, the student revolution in the 1960s made a strong impression in Norway. The latter offered an incentive to similar unrest in the Norwegian universities: American and Norwegian youngsters both turned against the new society of superabundance and its callous passivity and questioned the value of material comfort. Impressions of American feminism also fitted into this picture.

In 1968, the immense electoral support of the Republican team of Nixon and Agnew demonstrated to the world how irreconcilable were the differences. The tension had its grotesque release in the investigations climaxed by the Watergate affair in which, before the eyes of the entire world, the leading American spokesmen of "law and order" were exposed in public as simple criminals, together with a crowd of their helpers. The question was bound to arise whether, in the words of the Norwegian minister of foreign affairs twenty-five years before, the United States actually had the same ideas as the Norwegians about the meaning of democracy.

The internal circumstances would not have shaken Norwegian opinion so deeply if they had not at the same time manifested themselves in foreign politics.

Among the overwhelming majority of the Norwegian people there was a clear and strong repudiation of communism, both as a political system of coercion and as an ideological screen for old and well-known power politics. The net of assistance pacts and military bases which, from the 1950s onward, the United States built up around the Soviet Union and gradually also around Communist China, might appear as the necessary modern form of that American "bulwark against despotism" that was once praised by Garibaldi. But the individual foreign policy actions of the American government within this framework soon were bound to strengthen a suspicion that the encirclement of the Communist states was also intended to serve more egotistical aims. There was in Norway a keen interest in the liberated developing nations and a positive willingness to assist them. The American government displayed much less eagerness in that direction. Instead, it seemed to be the main concern of the United States everywhere to keep cooperative national regimes in power, although they might well be brutal dictatorships, if only they declared themselves to be anti-communist and gave a free hand and offered safe working conditions to American capital.

This policy was demonstrated time and again in the Far East and Latin America, sometimes in crass forms. In Europe, the United States turned out to be the faithful support of coercive regimes in Greece and Portugal. Norwegians with their strong sympathies in the Spanish Civil War felt particularly revolted by American cooperation with General Franco. Behind this policy loomed the economic-military system of power which President Eisenhower himself had warned against in his farewell address and which obviously was beyond real parliamentary control. Norwegians were indignant when in 1960 an American U-2 espionage plane, shot down by the Russians over Siberia with grave international repercussions, proved to have been on its way to a Norwegian airfield without Norwegian permission. American military and intelligence leaders often seemed to carry on a foreign policy of their own, independent of the American government, through the CIA, the giant secret organization established under President Truman. As early as 1940 a sober-minded American observer had prophesied that the United States might "prove to be the most conservative force in the twentieth century." Such fears now seemed to be vindicated.

To a great many Norwegians, the American war in Vietnam offered further proof of this development. The events in South-East Asia did not arouse in Norway the frantic anti-Americanism that was typical of contemporary Sweden. Too many Norwegians knew that even Communist power policies were involved. But as the war dragged on and the details were divulged, the action evoked an increasing aversion in Norway, not only because of the brutality of the warfare itself with its reminiscences of Hiroshima and the cynical American cooperation with the ruling clique in Saigon, but because of the revelation of the dishonorable political plots behind the decisions in Washington.

Demonstrations against the United States now became everyday events in the streets of Oslo as they did in most of the capitals of Europe. When in 1973 the Nobel Peace prize was awarded to Secretary of State Henry Kissinger for the "peace" in Vietnam, repugnance in Norway was rampant far beyond the circles of the professional haters of America. The reaction reached a new climax in 1973 when the military coup took place in Chile and a serious attempt at social reform was quelled in blood with the manifest assistance of American capital interests.

It is understandable that many Norwegians felt threatened by such events. As members of NATO, they might ask themselves how much liberty of action might be allowed to the individual small states even in other parts of the globe. As early as 1961 the new Socialist People's party (a splinter group of Labor, but clearly non-Communist) had elected to Parliament two representatives committed by the party platform to vote against NATO membership; the number of representatives increased in following elections. The anxiety was not only linked to considerations of military policy but to the entire recent development of technology, which so obviously was getting out of control. In 1962 the Nobel committee granted the Peace prize to the American Linus C. Pauling. He had earlier been honored with the Nobel prize in chemistry. Now the

Norwegian committee recognized his fight against the spread of atomic power.

Perhaps even more momentous were hesitations in the field of economy. In dollars and cents, American pressure on Norwegian economic life was not yet too threatening. But American capital was invested largely in companies that were already under foreign control. It made its power directly felt in several key industries and indirectly in others, allegedly in ways that did not necessarily serve Norwegian interests. Such ideas were bound to gain force when, in the 1970s, immense reservoirs of oil and natural gas were discovered in the Norwegian parts of the North Sea. At one blow, little Norway became a part of the great capitalist game of power, whether the Norwegians liked it or not. The multinational giant concerns became an integral part of Norwegian life. It was uncertain to what extent they could be kept in check by a small nation.

Many international problems were placed in a new light by the changed situation of the 1970s. There was in Norway a growing skepticism toward the ideology of unlimited economic growth with its steadily increasing demands of production and its somber side effects on the conditions of human life. Frequently, Norwegian doubts borrowed their arguments from American self-criticism. Demands for a reduction of the tempo of development, a cry for decentralization and protection of the fringe districts, and a movement "back to the grass roots" are typical trends of Norwegian thought during these years, often based on ecological considerations.

These currents demonstrated their unexpected strength when in 1973 Norway by plebiscite refused to join the European Common Market. The decision was made on political and economic grounds, but it tied up with a number of cultural problems of wider scope and led to serious disunion within the old political parties. The movement itself was not anti-American, but unavoidably it strengthened resistance against that international form of civilization which had its main exponent in the industrial giant of the West.

The result of all these interacting forces was, in the 1960s and early 1970s, a Norwegian debate about the United States and its relation to Norway which has no earlier parallel either in extent or in intensity. Old man Crèvecoeur's words about America's "close affinity with our present time" proved to be true once again. The problem was discussed in hundreds of Norwegian articles, pamphlets, and books which cannot be surveyed here. Moreover, much of the material was linked to the Vietnam War, which is now a thing of the past. But the general attitudes are revealed even in select samples.

In this discussion, many of the features may remind the reader of the past, even the distant past. Quite a few of the charges that are now again being directed against the United States have been customary in public debate, in and outside of Norway, at least from the middle of the nineteenth century. Nevertheless, a few things have changed. Only to a small extent does discussion in the 1970s build on loose rumors and debatable information. Overwhelmingly, observers now operate with generally known facts, more often than not culled from American sources and frequently official. Differences of opinion largely appear in combination and evaluation. Much less than before, discussion hinges on individual American phenomena. Rather, there is a confrontation of general attitudes and acceptance or nonacceptance of universal trends of development. Here, today as always, judgment often is bound to be emotional and existential, reflecting a personal standard of values and a feeling of solidarity with different human and social groups.

There are definite differences of opinion based on age. The negative view prevails among the young, who have no sentimental memories from the war and are only willing to base their judgment on their own observation and experience. The salient points of their attitude were clearly summarized in 1969 by one of the younger members of Parliament for the Labor party. In the main, his ideas are representative even after Vietnam. In his opinion, the United States is the dominant economic and military power in the present world and, at the same time, Norway's ally. The future of the Norwegians and everyone else is dependent on the United States, its development, and the direction of its power. Therefore, it is of decisive importance that in its policies, internal and external, America "has come to stand for actions and ideals which ought not to be ours," an industrial and technical growth in which Norway is not willing to participate and a cultural development which the Norwegians do not wish for themselves. A fight against the "American way of life" is a moral duty not only to the Norwegians but to mankind, not least to the poor nations on earth.

Behind this reasoning there is a sense of disappointment, even among the younger generation. Promises of the past are no longer being fulfilled; "Walt Whitman is weeping in his grave." Tunes from the American resistance movement in the 1960s resound in these exclamations, often combined with strong words, the use of old stereotypes, and sometimes a grotesque simplification. A young political scientist finds the present-day political alternatives to be an American world domination and "a world where injustice and hostility are done away with in the line of peace-loving socialist states."

But exaggeration does not invalidate the real arguments. In their discussions, the critics go far beyond general statements. They point to the average American's lack of understanding of other forms of society, combined with his willingness to exploit them economically. They refer to the stagnant political machinery of America, the impotence of the old progressivism, the criminality and lack of personal security, the "hidden violence" in the ghetto, and the callousness of the popular majority, who tolerate a glaring poverty in the midst of unparalleled riches. Above all, the critics maintain that the average American apparently has no understanding of the real motive powers in his own society and in the world and still meets problems with phrases about the self-made and strong individual, meaningless slogans out of the past.

Sometimes, but not often, such ideas are modified by the notion that, after all, these difficulties are not peculiar to the United States. One writer speaks of "our share in America's view of life" and "the fear of *America in ourselves.*" But most frequently America is singled out as something extraordinary, without a real counterpart, sick and marked for ruin, and with little hope for the future. Once in a while, there is an optimistic word about the "black masses" and the radical youth that perhaps may save the world. But there is little conviction behind it. The idea of catastrophe predominates.

All the critics so far referred to more or less belong to the left side of the social spectrum, even if only a few of them are Communists. The most positive judgments come from the Conservative side. Books dealing with America are published by a group which is closely tied to Norwegian industry and is more extremely rightist than even the Conservative party. Both with regard to the United States and to the world in general, this group is far more pleased with the situation than are their opponents. Some of its members just repeat Conservative propaganda. Allegedly, the real threat to the United States is not conditions in the country itself but radicals. The nation can only be saved by "free enterprise," law and order, and by President Nixon who, with his new spirit, will "give the Americans more for which they can respect their country" (printed in 1973).

Here again, historical stereotypes are being mobilized, as was the case on the opposite side. There is a willingness to excuse and to interpret everything in the best way possible: the United States is supporting the authoritarian governments of the world "with a bad conscience." At the same time, there is little understanding of the real interests of the common man in the underdeveloped countries. The goal of American politics is "the welfare and liberty of the nations on one side and America's self-interest on the other," and, "largely speaking," these two motives happily coincide.

This is only one side of the coin, however. Several Conservative writers are more than open to the dark aspects of present-day America, both in its internal and foreign policy, and often point to the same frightening features that are being underscored on the radical side. Not rarely, such elements are depicted in somber colors. If, even so, the story somehow has come to a happy end, it is due to a kind of teleological willingness to believe, not unknown in the history of economic liberalism. In the United States as in Norway, technical development is the encouraging revolution of our time. Sooner or later it is going to create a new and unknown society with "more wealth and more leisure time," if only we have the patience to wait.

At bottom lies the conviction that liberty in the United States, as defined by Americans, is the real answer to all criticism, and that there should be no tactless questions about the real value and extent of this liberty for the common man of the 1970s. This attitude is expressed in a book written by the editor of a Norwegian Conservative paper. In his analysis of America, he uses the black colors more than most. But all this counts for little compared to that feeling of "sudden happiness" which often fills him when he is in the United States. There capitalism is still alive, "gives everybody a chance to become what they themselves wished to be," and, for the rest, "leaves people alone." Moreover, quite recently the capitalist system has been given a broadly democratic foundation by the sale of shares to the common man. A nation living up to such ideals surely is going to master its problems in the future.

In the world in which the majority of human beings are existing today, this optimism appears as even less convincing than the doomsday visions of the other side. But there is also an opinion which is less tied to extreme points of view. Its pictures have more shades, and not all of them are negative.

The older generation, with its traditional faith in America's future, still at this late hour was represented by Halvdan Koht. In 1964 the first atom-propelled American cargo ship arrived in Oslo; it was named the *Savannah* like the first steam-propelled American ship to visit the country in 1819. Koht at that time was ninety years of age and almost blind; he was led on board the ship by his grandchildren. He was overwhelmed by his impressions and dictated an article right away. He looked back over eighty years of American inventions. Memories were not all bright: both atomic power and mass media could "hit both ways." But Koht preferred to think of the human creative power thus manifested, which had "pulled all nations on earth together more closely than ever." He insisted on believing in the power of good. Thus, he saw the *Savannah* as a hopeful message.

Four years later, a Norwegian journalist who knew America well, Arne Bonde, published a book called *USA—Plus/Minus*. Far more than Koht, he was marked by growing doubts about present-day America that were now habitual even among old friends of the United States. The material presented by him makes a terrifying effect by its kaleidoscopic absurdity. Most of the actual problems are analyzed in his book in their full gravity, sometimes to excess. Still, he sees reasons for optimism, above all in the American habit of self-scrutiny and in the dynamic and persistent attitude which, to him, is still a living force in most Americans.

Two solid Norwegian periodicals in 1969 and 1973 published special issues on America. The moderately conservative *Minerva's Kvartalsskrift* had articles by both Norwegian and American writers who expressed themselves with great caution; there were no cheap slogans. In their view, a new type of society may be in the offing in the United States, liberal in its main direction and with fewer reactionary tendencies. Here, too, self-criticism is pointed to as a positive sign, together with the free exchange of opinion. But whether such "hidden" forces may influence developments radically enough and rapidly enough must appear as uncertain.

The more radical _Internasjonal politikk_ used almost exclusively Norwegian experts for its special issue. Here, too, the writers saw in American opinion a dawning sense of something new, "different, important, and probably of a lasting nature." In the wake of Vietnam and Watergate, there is a healthy feeling that the United States has been "derailed," that the old national myths are today nothing but absurdities. America is marked by a new anxiety about mass media and their manipulation of opinion, energetic attempts at the solution of problems such as pollution, and a new realism in the face of its ethnic variety. American youth often look at their situation with fresh eyes.

But even here the question is being asked whether these attitudes and measures go far enough and are resorted to in time. Above all, the United States today raises the same essential question that perplexes urbanized Europe: whether the complacent middle class in the Western world of the 1970s is sufficiently interested in that really pluralistic society without which democracy today cannot survive, and whether that class might conceivably be willing to reduce its consumption of energy and cut down its living standard in the interest of other human groups, at home and abroad, now and in the future. Here, present-day America offers no answer.

Ingrid Semmingsen's _Rise of a World Power_ (1972) is well balanced without extreme opinions of any kind. But toward the end the author sums up "the problems of the society of superabundance" as they appear in all democratic, industrialized societies in the 1960s and, "in a particularly acute form," in the United States. Against these difficulties she raises "the American Dream," which has played such an immense part in American history, and asks what its chances of survival are under the new conditions. She points to the forces which in the past, again and again, have created usable forms of adaptation. Those forces are not defunct even today. But evidently our generation is facing crises of a new kind, in which the result must be uncertain. The practical idealism of individuals and the traditional openness in American society itself may once more lead to pragmatic and realistic solutions, both within America and in the world. But the final word is "perhaps."

Such doubtful and tentative hopes for the future of the United States are far away from the triumphant cries of the 1770s when the country made its entry on the world stage as "the vanguard of mankind." But a consistent development has taken us that far, on both sides of the ocean.

For geographical and historical reasons Norway was a late participant in the interplay and the exchange of values across the Atlantic. Its important contact with America has been limited to the last two centuries, and poverty long made connections tenuous. Nevertheless, during this period Norway shared in the most important American gifts to Europe. Emigration, immense compared to the size of the population and lasting for almost a century, made for contacts both wide and intimate.

The image of America thus created for a long time constituted the main link between the two countries. It was varied and filled with contrasts, as was America itself. Norway made few original contributions to its interpretation. But, largely speaking, in making up its mind about the United States, Norway was able to formulate its opinions in relative independence, in accordance with its own needs, prejudices, and predilections, and to use what it received in promotion of its own life.

In the beginning, hardly anything came across the ocean except ideas. But during the first century after 1776, their impact was impressive. With unusual clarity, Norway took its stand in favor of the radical American libertarian and equalitarian tradition against the conservative forces in state, society, and cultural life and turned it into a real factor in the development of Norwegian democracy.

With industrialization, the importance of such influences decreased beside the economic impact. In the course of a few decades, the United States became a part of Norway's everyday economic life and became one of the forces molding its very pattern of life. Insensibly, Norway thus became absorbed into the form of civilization typical of the twentieth century everywhere, and it turned its new knowledge to good use.

But at the same time, on both sides of the ocean the same problems arose: how to make expansive capitalism adapt itself to the demands of social responsibility and how to realize the ideas of liberty and equality to their full extent under the new conditions of life. Here, until the 1930s, the United States again was a bone of contention, but it also offered encouragement each time its reform movements seemed to move in step with similar forces in Norway. Relations during World War II and, even more, the military alliance of the 1940s were based on the hopeful assumption that Norway and the United States still shared their basic ideals to a considerable extent.

Such dreams during the recent decade have been rudely put to the test. In Norwegian minds, the high hopes of earlier generations have been replaced by a loss of confidence which Norway is today sharing with great parts of the Western world. The change makes a doubly strong impression because it reflects a similar conflict within America itself.

The opinion which the Norwegians are thus formulating about the United States and its future may seem to be of dubious general interest. They have no divinatory gifts. Even in practical fields their ideas may appear as irrelevant, at least at first. Most Norwegians probably are intent on maintaining the membership of their country in NATO, whatever the prophecies about America's future may be.

All the same, during the 1970s these ideas have acquired a range and taken on a human importance unknown in the earlier debates about America. The United States today is not just an immensely powerful nation. In its main economic, social, and cultural features, it represents with unusual clarity the general motive forces within that Western civilization which is taking shape in this century and is swiftly conquering the world. Much more than before, the development of America has become a road sign and a handwriting on the wall. The 4 million Norwegians have to ask about the direction of growth in the United States before they decide where to go themselves.

Two paramount problems are confronting the world today, both of them global in scope: (1) whether it will prove possible to control and direct the new powers of production so as to make them serve the well-being of the many in accordance with sensible plans, as formulated most clearly and comprehensively by socialism; and (2) whether such control and direction can be organized without that loss of spiritual freedom that most often has been associated with communism. Solutions and priorities are bound to vary in various parts of the world according to conditions and traditions. But most Norwegians may choose a road in the middle. They are apt to reject the sharp polarization typical of the largest of the NATO powers. They prefer trying to combine features from both sides. Without denying their membership in the world, they are also intent on judging critically that very civilization which today often reaches them under an American trademark. They are concerned with basic values, not only in the Norwegian but also in the European cultural tradition.

Whether such ideas may prove to be of any avail in the world that is now arising before the eyes of the present generation is not going to be decided by the Norwegians, but in great measure by the development of the United States. Here everything is hanging in the air. America today shows the world a changeable and restless face, as it often did in the past. Not infrequently, beneath this Janus-mask has lately been glimpsed the face of Medusa with its congealed look, distorted and distressful, a warning that the end of the world in the literal sense is not just a piece of mythology.

It is their own destiny which the Europeans thus, with fear and doubt, are trying to discern in the play of features in America's varying face. It must add to their anxiety, and to their feeling of responsibility as well, that no longer are they looking into a strange and irrelevant countenance, as they did one hundred years ago, but on the contrary must recognize in the Americans the dominant features of their own faces.

§

Selected Bibliography

The listing is mainly limited to literature in English with immediate relevance to the subject. In addition are included a few items of more general importance.

Albeck, G. "Amerika og Danmark: En oversigt." *Amerika och Norden.* Stockholm: Utg. L. Aahnebrink, 1964, 29-53. (Publ. of the Nordic Assn. for Am. Studies 1.)

Allen, H. C. *Great Britain and the United States. A History of Anglo-American Relations (1783-1952).* London, 1954.

Andersen, A. W. "American Labor Unrest in Norway's Press: The Haymarket Affair and the Pullman Strike." *The Swedish Pioneer Historical Quarterly* 25 (1974), 208-219.

_____. "American Politics in 1880: Norwegian Observations." *Scandinavian Studies* 40 (1968), 233-247.

_____. "Knut Hamsun's America." *Studies of the Norwegian-American Historical Association* 23 (1967), 175-203.

Anderson, C. L. *Poe in Northlight. The Scandinavian Response to His Life and Work.* Durham, N.C., 1973.

_____. *The Swedish Acceptance of American Literature.* Stockholm, 1957.

Bailey, Th. A. *The Policy of the US toward the Neutrals, 1917-1918.* Baltimore, 1942. Norway, p. 102-135.

Berg, R. G. *Moderna amerikaner.* Stockholm, 1925. Postscript, 149-186: Nordamerikansk litteratur i Sverige.

Bjork, K. *Saga in Steel and Concrete: Norwegian Engineers in America.* Northfield, Minn., 1947.

Blegen, Th. C., ed., *Land of Their Choice: The Immigrants Write Home.* Minneapolis, Minn., 1955.

_____. *Norwegian Migration to America.* 2 vols. Northfield, Minn., 1931-1940.

Bloch-Hoell, N. "The Impact in Norway of American Religious Dissent." *Contagious Conflict,* ed. A.N.J. den Hollander, Leiden, 1973, 214-232.

_____. "Norwegian Ideas of American Christianity." *Americana Norvegica* 4 (Oslo, 1973), 69-88.

_____. *The Pentecostal Movement.* Oslo, 1964.

Bowman, S., ed. *Edward Bellamy Abroad: An American Prophet's Influence.* New York, 1962.

Boyesen, E. "Hartvig Nissen and American Educational Reform." *Americana Norvegica* 1. Philadelphia, 1966, 161-179.

Curti, Merle. *American Philanthropy Abroad: A History.* Rutgers University Press, 1963.

_____. "The Reputation of America Overseas (1776-1860)." *American Quarterly* 1 (1949), 58-82. Repr. in Curti, *Probing Our Past,* New York, 1955 and 1962.

_____ and K. Birr. "The Immigrant and the American Image in Europe, 1860-1914." *Mississippi Valley Historical Review* 37 (1950), 203-230.

Danton, J. P. *United States Influence on Norwegian Librarianship, 1890-1940.* Berkeley and Los Angeles, Calif., 1957. (Univ. of Calif. Publ. in Librarianship II/1.)

Echeverria, D. *Mirage in the West: A History of the French Image of American Society to 1815.* Princeton, N.J., 1957.

Elovson, H. *Amerika i svensk litteratur 1750-1820.* Lund, 1930.

Fogdall, S.J.M.P. *Danish-American Diplomacy 1776-1920.* Iowa City [1923]. (Univ. of Iowa Studies in the Social Sciences VIII, 2.)

Geis, G. L. *American Motion Pictures in Norway: A Study in International Mass Communications.* Diss. University of Wisconsin, 1953, mimeographed.

Gjertsen, Ö. "The Seventh-Day Adventist Church in Norway: A Factual Account." *Americana Norvegica* 2. Philadelphia, 1968, 74-93.

Gvaale, G. H. *O. E. Rölvaag, nordmann og amerikanar.* Oslo, 1962.

Haugen, Einar. *The Norwegian Language in America: A Study in Bilingual Behavior.* 2 vols. Philadelphia, 1953. Repr., 1970. (Publ. of the American Institute, University of Oslo.)

Haugen, Eva L. and I. Semmingsen. "Peder Anderson of Bergen and Lowell: Artist and Ambassador of Culture." *Americana Norvegica* 4 (Oslo 1973), 1-29.

Heindel, R. H. *The American Impact on Great Britain, 1898-1914: A Study of the United States in World History.* Philadelphia, 1940.

Hovde, B. J. *Diplomatic Relations of the United States with Sweden and Norway 1814-1905.* Iowa City, 1921. (University of Iowa Studies in the Social Sciences VII, 4.)

_____. "Notes on the Effects of Emigration upon Scandinavia." *Journal of Modern History* 6 (1934), 253-279.

Hyman, H., ed. *Heard Round the World: The Impact Abroad of the Civil War.* New York, 1969.

Jantz, H. "Amerika im deutschen Dichten und Denken." *Deutsche Philologie im Aufriss,* hg. W. Stammler, 3, 2. Ausg. Berlin, 1962, 309-372.

Johns, B. S. "William Dean Howells and Björnstjerne Björnson: A Literary Relationship." *Americana Norvegica* 2. Philadelphia, 1968, 94-117.

Johnsen, A. O. "Björnson's Reaction to Emigration." *Publ. of the Norw.-Am. Historical Assn.* 6 (1931), 133-145.

Knaplund, P. "H. Tambs Lyche: Propagandist for America." *Norwegian-American Studies* 24 (1970), 102-111.

Koht, Halvdan. *The American Spirit in Europe: A Survey of Transatlantic Influences.* Philadelphia, 1949. Repr., 1970. (Publ. of the American Institute, University of Oslo.)

_____. "Bernadotte and Swedish-American Relations, 1810-1814." *Journal of Modern History* 16 (1944), 265-285.

_____. *Education of an Historian.* New York, 1957.

Larson, H. and E. Haugen. "Björnson and America—A Critical Review." *Scandinavian Studies and Notes* 13 (1933-1935), 1-12.

Lieberman, S. *The Industrialization of Norway, 1800-1920.* Oslo, 1970.

Mannsaaker, J. *Emigrasjon og dikting. Utvandringa til Nord-Amerika i norsk skjönnlitteratur.* Oslo, 1971.

Morison, S. E. *The European Discovery of America: The Northern Voyages A.D. 500-1600.* New York, 1971.

Öksnevad, R. *U.S.A. in Norwegian Literature: A Bibliography.* Oslo, 1950.

Ore, Ö. "Brother Ebben in His Native Country." *Norw.-Am. Studies and Records* 17 (1952), 36-46.

Paulson, A. C. "Björnson and the Norwegian-Americans, 1880-81." *Norw.-Am. Studies and Records* 5 (1930), 84-109.

Qualey, C. C. "Jörgen Gjerdrum's Letters from America, 1874-75." *Norw.-Am. Studies and Records* 11 (1940), 82-97.

Reinert, O. "The Perplexed Promise: The Image of the United States in Two Popular Norwegian Magazines, 1835-1865." *Americana Norvegica* 2. Philadelphia, 1968, 34-73.

Rémond, R. *Les Etats-Unis devant l'opinion française, 1815-1852.* These, Paris, 1962. (Cahiers de la Fondation nationale des sciences politiques, 116-117.)

Riste, Olav. "An Idea and a Myth: Roosevelt's Free Ports Scheme for North Norway." *Americana Norvegica* 4 (Oslo, 1973), 379-397.

_____. *The Neutral Ally: Norway's Relations with Belligerent Powers in the First World War.* Oslo, 1965.

Runeby, N. *Den nya världen och den gamla: Amerikabild och emigrationsuppfattning i Sverige 1820-1860.* Uppsala, 1969.

Scott, Fr. D. "American Influences in Norway and Sweden." *The Journal of Modern History* 18 (1946), 37-47.

_____. "Sören Jaabæk, Americanizer in Norway: A Study in Cultural Interchange." *Studies and Records of the Norw.-Am. Hist. Assn.* 17 (1952), 84-107.

_____. *The United States and Scandinavia.* Cambridge, Mass., 1950.

Semmingsen, I. *Dröm og daad: Utvandringen til Amerika.* Oslo, 1975.

_____. "Emigration and the Image of America in Europe." In *Immigration and American History: Essays in Honor of Th. C. Blegen.* Minneapolis, Minn., 1961, 26-54.

_____. *Veien mot vest: Utvandringen fra Norge.* 2 vols. Oslo, 1942-1950.

Skard, S. *American Studies in Europe: Their History and Present Organization.* 2 vols. Philadelphia, 1958. (Publ. of the American Institute, University of Oslo.) Bibliography, pp. 660-668. Abbreviated ed.: *The American Myth and the European Mind.* Philadelphia, 1961. Repr., 1964.

_____. "Hemingway in Norway." In *The Literary Reputation of Hemingway in Europe.* Paris and New York, 1965, 127-149.

_____. "The Image of America in Europe." In *American Civilisation: An Introduction,* ed. A.N.J. den Hollander and S. Skard. London, 1968, 455-473; bibliography, 502-508.

_____. *The Study of American Literature.* Philadelphia, 1949.

Steenstrup, P. Chr. "Ludvig Kristensen Daa and the USA." *Americana Norvegica* 1. Philadelphia, 1966, 45-96.

Stonehill, A. *Foreign Ownership in Norwegian Enterprises.* Oslo, 1965. (Samfunnsökonomiske studier 14.)

Storing, P. E. "United States' Recognition of Norway in 1905." *Americana Norvegica* 2. Philadelphia, 1968, 160-190.

Sveino, P. "Kristofer Janson and His American Experience." *Americana Norvegica* 3 (Oslo, 1971), 88-104.

Torfason, Thormod. *A History of Ancient Vinland.* Transl. by Ch. G. Herbermann. New York, 1891.

Tvitekkja, O. *Hans Tambs Lyche and America: His Image of It and How He Was Influenced by American Ideas.* Thesis, University of Oslo, mimeographed. Oslo, 1973.

Udgaard, N. M. *Great Power Politics and Norwegian Foreign Policy. A Study of Norway's Foreign Relations November 1940-February 1948.* Oslo, 1973.

Voyages to Vinland. The First American Saga. Transl. E. Haugen. New York, 1942.

Weibull, J. and E. W. Fleisher. *Viking Times to Modern.* Stockholm, 1954.

Willey, N. L. "Wergeland and Emigration to America." *Scandinavian Studies* 16 (1940), 121-127.

Williams, Francis. *The American Invasion.* London, 1962.

Index of Names

CONTRIBUTIONS IN AMERICAN STUDIES
SERIES EDITOR: **Robert H. Walker**

Visions of America: Eleven Literary Historical Essays
Kenneth S. Lynn

The Collected Works of Abraham Lincoln, Supplement 1832-1865
Roy P. Basler, Editor

Art and Politics: Cartoonists of the *Masses* and *Liberator*
Richard Fitzgerald

Progress and Pragmatism: James, Dewey, Beard, and the American Idea
of Progress
David W. Marcell

The Muse and the Librarian
Roy P. Basler

Henry B. Fuller of Chicago: The Ordeal of a Genteel Realist in Ungenteel
America
Bernard R. Bowron, Jr.

Mother Was a Lady: Self and Society in Selected American Children's
Periodicals, 1865-1890
R. Gordon Kelly

The *Eagle* and Brooklyn: A Community Newspaper, 1841-1955
Raymond A. Schroth, S. J.

Black Protest: Issues and Tactics
Robert C. Dick

American Values: Continuity and Change
Ralph H. Gabriel

Where I'm Bound: Patterns of Slavery and Freedom in Black American
Autobiography
Sidonie Smith

William Allen White: Maverick on Main Street
John D. McKee

American Studies Abroad
Robert H. Walker, Editor

In the Driver's Seat
Cynthia Golomb Dettelbach

The United States in Norwegian History
Sigmund Skard

PUBLICATIONS OF THE AMERICAN INSTITUTE UNIVERSITY OF OSLO

Halvdan Koht: *The American Spirit in Europe. Survey of Transatlantic Influences.* ix, 289 pp. (Philadelphia, Pa., 1949). Reprint 1970.

Einar Haugen: *The Norwegian Language in America. A Study in Bilingual Behavior.*
Vol. I: The Bilingual Community. xiv, 317 pp.
Vol. II: The American Dialects of Norwegian. vii, 377 pp. (Philadelphia, Pa., 1953). 2nd edition, in one volume. xxvii, 699 pp. (Bloomington, Ind., 1970).

Sigmund Skard: *American Studies in Europe. Their History and Present Organization.*
Vol. I: The General Background, The United Kingdom, France, and Germany. Pp. 1-358.
Vol. II: The Smaller Western Countries, The Scandinavian Countries, The Mediterranean Nations, Eastern Europe, International Organization, and Conclusion. Pp. 359-736 (Philadelphia, Pa., 1958).

Americana Norvegica. Norwegian Contributions to American Studies.
Vol. I. Editors: Sigmund Skard and Henry H. Wasser. 340 pp. (Philadelphia, Pa., 1966).
Vol. II. Editor: Sigmund Skard. Editorial Committee: Ingvald Raknem, Georg Roppen, Ingrid Semmingsen. 357 pp. (Philadelphia, Pa., 1968).
Vol. III. Studies in Scandinavian-American Interrelations Dedicated to Einar Haugen. Editors: Harald S. Naess and Sigmund Skard. Editorial Committee: Ingvald Raknem, Ingrid Semmingsen, Orm Överland. 390 pp. (Oslo, 1971).
Vol. IV. Norwegian Contributions to American Studies Dedicated to Sigmund Skard. Editor: Brita Seyersted. Editorial Committee: Helge Normann Nilsen, Orm Överland, Ingrid Semmingsen. xiv, 442 pp. (Oslo, 1973).

Jan W. Dietrichson: *The Image of Money in the American Novel of the Gilded Age.* 417 pp. (Oslo and New York, 1969).

Per Seyersted: *Kate Chopin. A Critical Biography.* 247 pp. (Oslo and Baton Rouge, La., 1969).

Per Sveino: *Orestes A. Brownson's Road to Catholicism.* 340 pp. (Oslo and New York, 1970).

Orm Överland: *The Making and Meaning of an American Classic. James Fenimore Cooper's* The Prairie. 207 pp. (Oslo and New York, 1973).

Dorothy Burton Skaardal: *The Divided Heart. Scandinavian Immigrant Experience through Literary Sources.* 394 pp. (Oslo and Lincoln, 1974).

Sigmund Skard: *The United States in Norwegian History.* (Oslo and Westport, Conn., 1976).